THE

GOSPEL OF KNEE-SUS

AND

RELIGION OF

VICTIMANITY

Copyright 2019

Taleeb Starkes

***

*DEDICATED TO THE CHURCH OF THE
ETERNAL VICTIM*

In the eBook, the sources (nearly two hundred) are hyperlinked, and Knee-sus' words are red. In this book, Knee-sus' words are in a bold, black font.

Please pardon the crossed-out Freudian slips within this scroll.

TABLE OF CONTENTS

CHAPTER I

Revelation Replaces Genesis

[1] ~~In the beginning, was the Word.~~ In the beginning of the National Football League's (NFL) 2016 season was the Word.

[2] And the Word was victimhood in the flesh who dwelled amongst NFL players as a declining quarterback.

[3] And the Word wasn't with God Goodell, the supreme deity of the NFL.

[4] In those days, God Goodell was uneasy with the Word. However, his uneasiness was a sharp pivot from the feelings he possessed for the Word before the 2016 season.

[5] In 2012, as a second-year, backup quarterback, the Word was highly favored by both God Goodell and the sports media. That year, he unexpectedly led his team (San Francisco 49ers) to the NFL's ultimate game (Super Bowl) and came within five yards of winning it.

⁶ Although his spectacular Super Bowl feat ended in defeat, he didn't feel defeated. *"It's good to get the experience,"* said the Word postgame.ⁱ *"We should have won that game regardless, though."*

⁷ He promised to improve for the following 2013 season and spent the off-season with the Super Bowl in his crosshairs. The loss was motivation to do more than just reach the Super Bowl; he wanted to win it.

⁸ And when the 2013 regular season ended (which was his first full season as starting quarterback), the off-season's Super Bowl goal was within reach. He had resiliently willed his team back to the National Football Conference's (NFC) championship game. Unfortunately, he stumbled one win short of the anticipated Super Bowl return.

⁹ Still, within a mere two years (2012 and 2013), the Word had taken his team to two NFC championship games and one Super Bowl. God Goodell was well pleased with him.

10 In 2013, he received the NFL's *"Greatness on the Road"* award for demonstrating the best performance in a regular season road game. [ii]

11 Additionally, ESPN, the U.S.-based sports network, which is considered the worldwide leader in sports coverage, awarded the Word its 2013 ESPY award a.k.a. *"Breakthrough Athlete of the Year"* award. [iii]

12 It was evident that the sky was his ceiling.

13 Standing at 6 feet, 4 inches tall, and having the ability to make plays with his arm or legs in the read-option offense, the Word became the NFL's poster boy for the evolution of the quarterback position.

14 He possessed a cannon arm with rumored 60-mile-per-hour spiral passes, and the speed of Hermes; speed powered by feet that were the color of fine pizza dough baked in a furnace.

15 And when he called plays at the line of scrimmage, his voice rang with the sound of many ~~waters~~ Gatorades.

16 The Word scored touchdowns so frequently that he developed a signature touchdown celebration. The celebration was a graceful air kiss on his flexed biceps.

¹⁷ Defensive coordinators around the NFL were on notice that this young phenom would be a difficult force to scheme against for years to come.

¹⁸ One ex-NFL quarterback turned NFL analyst, prophesized that the Word *"could be one of the greatest quarterbacks ever."*[iv] And GQ magazine put more butter on his biscuit by calling him, *"Mentally and spiritually, old-school, with the Knute Rockne-ish non-self-regarding self-regard of a faceless soldier in a Crusade."*[v]

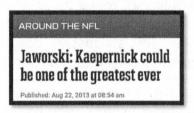

AROUND THE NFL

Jaworski: Kaepernick could be one of the greatest ever

Published: Aug 22, 2013 at 08:54 am

¹⁹ His team's ownership also recognized that he was a valuable commodity with still untapped potential. Which is why in 2014, the storied franchise rewarded him with a six-year contract extension worth up to $126 million[vi] – including $61 million in potential guarantees and a $12 million signing bonus.

²⁰ Having the Word financially-secured at the helm as the team's franchise quarterback generated championship expectations from the adoring media and fans. His supercalifragilisticexpialidocious (I like that term) 2012 and 2013 seasons were construed as harbingers of the team's future.

[21] But, the 2014 team apparently didn't receive that optimistic memo regarding the supercalifragilisticexpialidocious (OK, I love that term) expectations. They struggled throughout the 2014 season and finished with as many wins as losses: 8-8. For the first time in four years, the 49ers didn't make the playoffs.

[22] Losing was an anomaly for the Word. He had experienced success at every level of athletic competition. In high school, his insatiable desire to succeed propelled him to receive a full, Division I, NCAA (National Collegiate Athletic Association) sports scholarship — despite being overlooked by most major colleges. It's noteworthy that only roughly two-percent of high school athletes annually win sports scholarships. [vii]

[23] The Word also played baseball. And while in college, his 94-miles per hour fastball put him on the radar of the Chicago Cubs, a Major League Baseball team. In 2009, the Cubs drafted the college junior as a pitcher. He declined their job offer. Football was and had always been his first love. Even as far back as the fourth-grade, football was his envisioned career. The fourth-grader put pencil to paper and projected:

"I hope I go to a good college in football then go to the pros and play on the Niners or the Packers, even if they aren't good in seven years." [viii]

24 Through sacrifice, perseverance, and a winning attitude, his dream was actualized. However, the dream slowly became a nightmare during the team's subpar 2014 season. The Word's discomfort with losing gave way to frustration that sometimes appeared on the playing field. He would unwisely do or say anything to gain a competitive edge.

25 He once got into a dust-up with an opposing defensive player and reportedly called the player (who was black) the N-Word.

26 The eyebrow-raising act turned out to be a costly lesson in sportsmanship and anger-management. God Goodell punished him with an $11,000 fine.

> **Race Matters: Biracial 49er's QB Colin Kaepernick Fined $11,000 For Using N-Word On The Field During Game**
>
> Posted on September 22, 2014 - By **Bossip Staff**

27 The black media also chided the Word —

albeit cunningly. They didn't approve of him using that racial epithet even though he's half-black. One of their headlines deliberately called him *"Biracial."* [ix] Any other time, they called him black. The racial jab was a subtle message to the Word that his half-white privilege had restrictions. Usage of the N-word was assuredly an uppermost violation.

[28] No problem! The Word developed other methods to alleviate frustration with losing while getting into his opponent's head.

[29] Before a 2015 preseason game against the Houston Texans, he shamelessly used an image of recent flash floods (that ravaged Houston and killed two people) to trash-talk Houston Texans' fans. The image, which he posted onto his social media account, had the caption, *"I warned you the #7tormsComing!!! #Houston."* [x] The Word was determined to capitalize on the calamity and not let any of it waste.

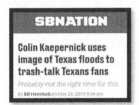

[30] The backlash was immediate. His idea to use a disaster to antagonize opponents was

disastrous. And though this unsportsmanlike conduct didn't cost him financially (via fine), his public image paid a cost. He eventually apologized and deleted the insensitive post.

[31] If only he could've deleted his team's entire 2015 season as easily. Their losing trend from 2014 had parachuted into 2015 at free fall speed.

[32] Naturally, there was plenty of blame for this dire reality, but the Word was inescapably a primary reason. He was failing to live up to the expectations bestowed upon him.

[33] In 2015, he posted career lows in nearly every major statistical category.[xi] His averages of 0.75 touchdowns and 0.625 interceptions per game were detrimental drop-offs from 2013 when he averaged 1.3 touchdowns per game and 0.5 interceptions. [xii] Fox Sports reported:

"Kaepernick had a defense-adjusted yards above replacement — Football Outsiders' ultimate value quotient — of minus-182, 35th in the NFL. By all metrics, he was one of the worst quarterbacks in the league. These numbers look even worse when you consider that the 49ers went to a single-read offense for Kaepernick after his terrible four-interception performance against the Arizona Cardinals in Week 3." [xiii]

[34] The Word's performance had been so shoddy that Jerry Rice, the 49ers' Hall of Fame receiver, called for him to be benched *"to energize the team."* [xiv]

[35] The stats didn't lie. Defenses had learned his passing tendencies, schemed to handicap his legs, and he didn't adjust accordingly. In 2014, Steve Young, the 49ers' Hall of Fame quarterback and model mobile quarterback, proposed that the Word literally tie his legs in practice to become a better pocket quarterback. Young advised:

"He's going to have to tie his legs in training camp. Literally, he should tie his legs, physically, so he can't do anything but throw from the pocket." [xv]

[36] Young's insight was not heeded. Seemingly overnight, the conversation about the Word's career had switched from championships and Super Bowls to salvageability versus irreparability. The debate was endless.

[37] Nonetheless, there was one aspect of the Word's career that wasn't debatable — his inconsistent playmaking.

[38] NFL.com had begun to describe him as a *"regressing quarterback who has struggled not only with the rudimentary passing elements such as accuracy, anticipation, and*

touch, but also with protections, field vision and decision making." [xvi]

39 Sports Illustrated predicted[xvii] that the end was near for the Word because his *"flaws speak to an ill understanding of basic progression reads and coverage diagnostics."* Moreover, his *"poor understanding for why certain plays are called"* was problematic. The sports magazine also opined that the Word would too often *"look to abandon the pocket the instant he reaches the top of his dropback. Coaches hate this because it nullifies the play's route designs. It can also create pressure where none existed."* And when he did play with patience, Sports Illustrated noted, *"he has a tendency to be late with the ball or to flat-out leave open receivers untargeted."*

40 Halfway through the 2015 season, the glaring deficiencies led to the Word being demoted to a backup quarterback. As the starting quarterback, the team had only won two games out of eight (2-6) at that point. His replacement was a journeyman quarterback who hadn't started a game since 2013 and had a 5-22 record as a starter. Inserting an arguably inferior quarterback over the Word was desperate times calling for desperate measures.

[41] The 49ers finished the 2015 season with the worst record in the division and had twice the amount of losses over wins (5-11).

[42] Like 2014, their championship aspirations met an early expiration, and the playoff drought proceeded unimpeded. The head coach was fired, and other heads were expected to roll if the team didn't quickly re-establish a winning culture.

[43] The Word grasped that the ship was sinking, and he wasn't willing to play soothing music on the deck until it capsized. So, during the off-season, he requested a trade.[xviii] He sent out a distress signal for a team to come to his rescue. No one came. The SOS trade request had failed; leaving him woefully stuck on the Titanic.

[44] Going into the 2016 season, the Word remained uncertain about the 49ers' commitment to him. As the face of the organization, he felt that his ignominious benching in 2015 was not how a franchise quarterback should've been treated.

---

[45] Adding insult to his emotional injury, the new head coach mistreated him just as the former head coach had done. The latest mistreatment happened in training camp. The new head coach had audaciously forced the Word to compete[xix] for the starting quarterback position against the journeyman quarterback. What fools these mortals be! The Word had now been slapped twice in his face by two different head coaches, and he was tired of turning the other cheek.

SBNATION

Blaine Gabbert, Colin Kaepernick splitting snaps to start training camp

The 49ers quarterback competition begins on even ground.

By David Fucillo on July 31, 2016 10:48 am

[46] Not being handed the starting quarterback position really shocked him. Sure, his last couple of seasons were turbulent, but after hitting rock-bottom, up was the only direction. Also, the media had forecasted that this marriage between the Word and new head coach *"terrifies defensive coaches."*[xx]

[47] The marriage, as the media predicted, was indeed terrifying. However, it didn't terrify defensive coordinators; the Word was the one left shaking in horror. The beginning of the marriage had been rocky, and by training camp's end, he was the designated

backup quarterback. The so-called franchise quarterback would have to watch the 2016 preseason games from the bench. For the Word, quarterback life was becoming a b**ch! (bench!)

48 When his initial benching occurred in 2015, the head coach at the time described it to the media as a moment for the struggling quarterback to *"step back and breathe and look at things through a different lens."* [xxi]

49 The Word's sarcastic response to the head coach's comment was, ***"I'm not out of breath, so I don't understand that reference."***[xxii]

50 In hindsight, the head coach was correct. Being benched did give the Word invaluable time to *"step back and breathe and look at things through a different lens."* The coach's suggestion ultimately led to the Word stepping forward to a far more fruitful career path.

51 Pondering on the pine (bench) during that statistically disastrous 2015 season, allowed him to dissect and analyze his football future like a molecular scientist.

52 He cherished being the face of the franchise and wanted to maintain that status by any means necessary.

53 But being on the bench posed a serious threat to his reputation and earning capacity. Therefore, he had to find a way to regain relevancy, and just as importantly, maintain it.

54 Knowing that the bench limited his ability to make a direct impact on the football field, the Word had to somehow become impactful from the sideline.

55 And though he did not yet have an actual idea to put into practice, the Word knew that the idea had to be seismic. It had to shock and awe. It needed to be groundbreaking, and leave an impression that would distract the masses from the reality of his best years being behind him and career lodged in quicksand.

56 It wasn't until the 2016 season that the idea he had steadfastly meditated on finally manifested. And when it appeared, it descended upon him like a dove. The Word had received what can only be best described as a spiritual revelation.

57 The revelation instructed him to perform an act that would indeed allow him to utilize his flesh on the field (even if he's technically on the sideline) and dwelleth in the people's hearts and minds — all while diverting attention from his stalled career. It was perfection!

58 So let it be written, so let it be done!

59 Unbeknownst to the 49ers' organization, non-omniscient God Goodell, and media, the Word would strategically unveil the inspired act during his team's first 2016 preseason game.

60 However, no one had noticed it until the team's third preseason game; a game where he debuted off the bench and finished with two completions on six attempts for seventeen yards.

61 When the National Anthem began, and attendees stood for the American flag, the Word designedly did something else.

62 He defiantly broke away from the time-honored tradition of standing as a sign of respect and unceremoniously sat.

63 Yes! The Word sat on the bench (like Forrest Gump) throughout the National Anthem and ignored the Star-Spangled Banner as if it was momentary noise from a passing automobile.

64 Aftershocks from his polarizing gesture reverberated around the country and world. He, not his gameplay or lack thereof, was the subject of national and international headlines.

⁶⁵ This specific outcome was what his heart had desired. All eyes were on him similar to the name of Tupac's fourth album.ˣˣⁱⁱⁱ

⁶⁶ After the game, he unflinchingly explained his behavior to the media and framed it as a protest against racial oppression in the United States.

⁶⁷ Behold! *"I am not going to stand up to show pride in a flag for a country that oppresses black people and people of color. To me, this is bigger than football and it would be selfish on my part to look the other way. There are bodies in the street and people getting paid leave and getting away with murder."*ˣˣⁱᵛ

⁶⁸ The Word's voice had regained that familiar sound of many Gatorades, and his countenance was as the sun shineth in his strength. He mesmerized the media.

⁶⁹ Not only were they curious about his stance, but also the T-shirt that he wore for what would be known as his first sermon on the ~~soapbox~~ mount.

⁷⁰ His T-shirt featured communist dictator Fidel Castro; a tyrant who ruled the totalitarian, police-state of Cuba for nearly six decades and practically eliminated all political and civil rights.ˣˣᵛ Under his regime, where Afro-Cubans also greatly suffered, any conversations of racial equality were grounds for imprisonment.

71 Certainly, seeing the Word proudly wear a T-shirt that's decorated with a notorious oppressor's image (while propagating an anti-oppression stance) may appear hypocritical. However, one must look deeper, subterranean deeper! He was not hypocritical; he was keepin' it real!

72 O ye, of little faith. Pay attention to his eloquent explanation for wearing the authoritarian's picture:

"One thing Fidel Castro did do is they have the highest literacy rate because they invest more in their education system than they do in their prison system, which we do not do here even though we're fully capable of doing that." xxvi

73 Granted, it's demonstrably false that Cuba had the highest literacy rate. xxvii Also, his claim that Cuba invested ***"more in their education system than they do in their prison system"*** should have an asterisk.

For many generations of Cubans, the island itself has basically been a prison with indoctrination camouflaged as education. Armando Salguero, a Cuban-American journalist whose family was torn apart by Castro's draconian policies, responded to the Word's claim:[xxviii]

"[C]ould it be Cuba doesn't have to invest a lot in its prison system because, you know, dungeons and firing squads (El Paredon) are not too expensive to maintain?"

74 Nonetheless, the Word was simply trying to humanize the despot as any genuine bleeding-heart liberal would do. The true takeaway from his rebuttal is that criticizers need to open their hearts before opening their mouths!

75 Nearly a month after the Word passionately defended his T-shirt, Fidel Castro died. The T-shirt now doubled as a "rest in peace" shout-out to his dead homie.

76 The Word's curious choice of fashion wasn't new. Several weeks before he conspicuously copped a squat during the National Anthem, the Word practiced in socks adorned with cops depicted as pigs. The media didn't seem to care or didn't care to notice.

77 But after learning of the socks, the media again questioned him about his fashion sense. Unbothered by the retroactive question, the Word took the opportunity to re-enlighten them from the mount. He calmly clarified that the socks ~~were~~ weren't demonizing all cops, only the "rogue ones."[xxix] Those cops should also be *"put in a blanket"* and fried like bacon — as often chanted by anti-police allies.[xxx]

78 It was highly uncharacteristic for the media to overlook the Word's striking fashion statement in training camp. Their neglect to notice his statement-driven attire (that reflected his mindset) was yet another clear indication of how little attention was being paid to him those days as a backup quarterback.

79 Suffice it to say, the lack of attention flipped following his National Anthem gesture and post-gesture sermons. The Word's outfits, plus any accessories, became targets of intense media scrutiny.

80 He welcomed the scrutiny because his plan was coming to fruition. Throwing this ball of victimhood was just as beneficial as throwing an NFL football.

81 Hence, his powerful declaration that the National Anthem protest would continue until he felt like **"[the American flag] represents what it's supposed to represent."** *xxxi*

82 The Word's open-ended timetable signified an unapologetic commitment to his silent protest at the National Anthem and National Football League's expense.

83 He did not come to bring peace, but a sword!

84 And he waited until his team's final 2016 preseason game to fully insert the sword into the public's psyche. The hour was at hand to complete the revelation.

85 It was "Salute to the Military" day at the football stadium — a textbook time to steal the shine from the service members and place it onto himself.

86 During the National Anthem, the Word did not sit as he had done for the previous games. On that sacred day, September 1st, 2016, he abandoned sitting. In its place, he unveiled an evolved version of his symbolic protest. It was something that would undoubtedly define his mission and ~~bury~~ cement his football legacy.

87 He knelt on one knee.

88 Realize, dear reader, the protest gesture that he had divinely ~~concocted~~ received to captivate the sports world was only a means for him to reveal his true identity.

89 Yes, he was the Word. But after that Sunday, the world would know him by his Ethereal name: Knee-sus, the Bender of the Knee. ~~Hilarious~~ Holy be his name.

90 *"Verily, verily, I say unto thee... fight racial oppression of blacks by getting down on one knee,"* is what Knee-sus conveyed on that hallowed day without uttering a word.

91 Once again, the media were enchanted and eager to disseminate his message. Of course, their motive had nothing to do with any belief in his message. They only believed in the potential ad revenue from clicks and social media shares surrounding his message. He was their newest ~~profit~~ prophet just like Alexandria Casio-Cortez (the Democratic-Socialist Congresswoman) became in 2019.

92 Time Magazine quickly ~~exploited~~ chose him for its famous cover that read, *"The Perilous Fight."* The weekly news magazine said he was the *"obvious choice"*xxxii for the cover. It doesn't take Captain Obvious to explain why Knee-sus was the obviou$ choice.

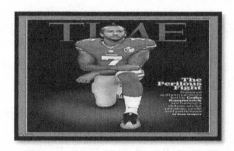

[93] Knee-sus' updated protest act of kneeling rapidly spread across the NFL; several players were inspired to follow his lead. Critics wondered if the degenerative brain disease called Chronic Traumatic Encephalopathy (CTE) had affected more NFL players than previously revealed. In their minds, CTE had to be the reason why these athletes were sabotaging the NFL — a league that financially allowed them to make tangible changes from their zip codes, area codes, and income brackets. Moreover, in a country that enables talent to be transformed into lucrative careers.

[94] Some players took a knee, sat on the bench, or stood with a raised fist. Knee-sus firstly asked the players *"to do nothing if they weren't going to take a knee."* He didn't want the message to be *"diluted, bastardized or overshadowed by people focusing on the*

method of protest rather than the message behind it." [xxxiii]

95 Eventually, he loosened the criterion, and other forms of protest became acceptable. Blessed were the troublemakers, as long as they were troublesome on his behalf.

96 And in a pandemic-like fashion, the kneeling spread beyond the NFL to other parts of the sports world.[xxxiv] Soccer star, Megan Rapinoe, kneeled in solidarity with Knee-sus as a *"nod to Kaepernick and everything that he's standing for right now."*[xxxv] Several high school athletes around the country did the same,[xxxvi] including a prep team[xxxvii] in San Francisco and an Oakland team that laid down with their hands up.[xxxviii] Some college football players raised their fists even though college teams aren't usually on the field during the National Anthem.[xxxix] In contrast, college marching bands are typically on the field during the National Anthem, which is how nineteen marching band members were able to take a knee.[xl] The spirit of Knee-sus also compelled a few college volleyball playersxli to join the knee-a-thon.[xlii]

97 For Knee-sus, the benefits of kneeling became incalculable. But one measurable benefit was how the bended-knee overshadowed his contorted quarterbacking in 2016. The fact that he ranked thirty (out of 34 players) in Football Outsiders' passing efficiency metrics[xliii] at the season's end (after regaining the starting job) was inconsequential to his followers and even teammates. His teammates still voted him as the 49er who best exemplified *"inspirational and courageous play"*[xliv] — in spite of his inspirational and courageous gameplay not translating onto the field.

[98] In week thirteen of the 2016 season, the inspiration and courage were particularly missing. It was Knee-sus' seventh consecutive start at quarterback, and the team was winless during that span.

[99] The coach had stayed the course and tolerated his erratic play. But this game forced the coach to exasperatingly take a timeout from his tolerance. Knee-sus was awful. Actually, he was godawful! So, the coach sent him back to Splinterville a.k.a. Pine Valley (the bench).

[100] His benching occurred in the fourth quarter; four quarters too late, as some people have surmised. When he was pulled from the game, his offensive output consisted of a single completion for four yards (out of five attempts). Yep, one, four-yard completion! He was also sacked five times.

101 Behold! Knee-sus had accumulated more sacks than passing yards. And though his stat line was pathetic, no one anticipated that it was historically pathetic.

102 He was the first quarterback in NFL history to throw for fewer than five yards in a game while being sacked five times.[xlv] That's a telling statistic. The NFL started compiling sacks in 1982.

Colin Kaepernick sets a new historical low, gets benched in loss to Bears

Dan Graf
Dec 9, 2016 at 12:57p ET

103 When asked about his historically abysmal performance and subsequent benching, Knee-sus was as cool as a cucumber and dismissively responded, ***"It wasn't something I expected."*** [xlvi]

104 Remember! 2016 was the Year of the Knee, the reason for the season. Hence, being benched (or not) was no longer an issue for Knee-sus. He had effectively ~~reinvented~~ revealed himself as something greater than the bench, team's win/loss record, or football.

105 He resumed the starting quarterback job for the remaining three games. The team finished the 2016 season with only two wins out of sixteen (2-14). The minuscule win tally was enough to secure sole possession of last place in the division and extend the playoff famine.

[106] And similar to what happened at the end of the 2015 season, heads rolled after that pitiful 2016 season. Not only was the coach fired after his lone season, but the general manager had succumbed to the guillotine as well.

[107] The Word didn't escape unscathed either. Earlier in season, the 49ers restructured his mega-contract and reduced the final four years to one, with a player's option.[xlvii] Even though his sixteen touchdowns and four interceptions in 2016 showed glimpses of that special 2012 and 2013 quarterback, the team knew that those 2016 numbers were deceptive. The touchdowns were mostly accumulated late in already decided games or "garbage time" — as it's called in the biz.

[108] The once-adoring sports media also weren't fooled by his misleading stat line. They had already dismissed him as a has been after universally praising him as an elite, futuristic quarterback in the 2012 and 2013 seasons.

[109] ESPN analyzed his last two seasons and reported, *"Since the start of the 2015 season, Kaepernick ranks last in the NFL*

among 35 qualified passers in off-target percentage (22.6). His completion percentage ranks No. 32 at 59.1."[xlviii]

110 From the franchise and media's perspective, the thrill was gone. In retrospect, the writing may have been on the wall as early as 2014 when his team began to slide into obscurity. At that time, NFL.com quietly questioned Knee-sus' viability:

"Quarterback is the most important job in sports because of everything that happens before the snap. If Kaepernick ever gets that religion, the Bay Area quarterback debate will be short-lived."

111 Knee-sus never did get *"that religion"* because he didn't need to get it. His calling was another religion; one based in victimhood. And that victim-centric religion inspired his pre-game, sideline pastime, which was more rewarding than anything he did during game time.

112 And that's why his timing to reveal himself on that blessed day in September couldn't have been more ideal.

113 Lo! In 2012 and 2013, he came giving the NFL and fans what they wanted (football) so that they would eventually want what he really came to give in 2016: The Knee.

CHAPTER II

Knee-groes

1 Behold! Just like Jesus of Nazareth was sent *"to the lost sheep,"*[xlix] as too, was Knee-sus of the Niners. He was sent to the lost black sheep. These black sheep are sacrificial lambs whose lives were lost at the hands of police. Their blood, especially the blood of the unarmed black sheep, is the secret sauce that powers his ministry.

2 Knee-sus stated that his mission is to fight for black people whose ***"bodies [are] in the street"*** due to police brutality and racial oppression. And during a sermon, he decried:

"As police officers continue to terrorize Black and brown communities, abusing their power, and then hiding behind their blue wall of silence, and laws that allow for them to kill us with virtual impunity, I have realized that our love, that sometimes manifests as Black-rage, is a beautiful form of defiance against a system that seeks to suppress our humanity--A system that wants us to hate ourselves." [l]

³ His love or **"Black-rage"** is directed at the system for allowing the perpetrators (police officers) to get away with murder while "getting paid leave." [li]

⁴ Therefore, as the ~~self-appointed~~ appointed shepherd of black sheep, Knee-sus religiously works to ensure that their deaths are not in vain. He doesn't even rest on the seventh day!

⁵ To him, their deaths are not only attention-worthy but knee-worthy. And that's why these black sheep are affectionately referred to as "Knee-groes."

⁶ Forty-year-old Terence Crutcher was one such designated Knee-groe. In September of the Year of the Knee, he was martyred by police in Tulsa, Oklahoma during a traffic incident.[lii] Crutcher was one of nineteen unarmed black sheep shot dead that year by police nationwide.[liii]

Terence Crutcher lying on the road

⁷ Since unarmed unequivocally means innocent to Knee-sus, he was vexed about Crutcher's death and used it to reaffirm his mission publicly. He remarked:

"This is a perfect example of what this is about. It will be very telling about what happens to the officer that killed him." [liv]

8 The incident sparked protests. Observe! Whenever Knee-groes are martyred, a critical aspect of Knee-sus' ministry is invoked: the knee-jerk reaction.

9 A rush to judgment is vital. Time isn't wasted on fact-finding or judging each occurrence individually on a case-by-case basis. Logical approaches are exercises in futility!

10 During these tragedies, patience is not a virtue; patience is a problem. Knee-sus wants swift action in the form of protests, rallies, hashtags, and social media activism.

11 Cops who kill Knee-groes, regardless of the circumstances, are automatically deemed guilty and doubly guilty if it's an unarmed Knee-groe. "Unarmed black male" is a label that immediately implies officer wrong-doing.

12 A day after Terence Crutcher was martyred, the body of a Chicago teenager was discovered burning in a fifty-five-gallon trash can. [lv] Fifteen-year-old Demetrius Griffin Jr., who often walked the neighbors' dogs, and faithfully honored his curfew, was charred beyond recognition. Dental records were used to identify him. Rumors persisted that the high school freshman was killed for refusing to join the local gang and gang initiation. Two years after his callous murder, which should've been exempted from the *"no snitching"* attitude that plagues inner-cities, the case remained open with no arrests or convictions. And, no bended-knee or compassionate commentary from Knee-sus.

¹³ Inquiring minds may wonder why there was no bended knee from Knee-sus. Well, the answer is simple. When it comes to receiving Knee-sus' salvation, many blacks are ~~culled~~ called, but the chosen are few.

¹⁴ Lest ye forget! When Knee-sus said, ***"To me, this is bigger than football and it would be selfish on my part to look the other way,"*** ^{lvi} he was only speaking about his chosen flock: Knee-groes. The onlooker must overstand (not understand) the distinction between Knee-groes and non-Knee-groes.

¹⁵ Anyone with at least one functioning eye (even if that eye is jaundiced) should be able

to see that Knee-sus undeniably *"look[s] the other way"* when it comes to the thousands of black homicide victims killed yearly by black perpetrators.

16 In urban America, where pervasive violence characteristically litters the landscape, even at wakes and vigils, blacks who are killed by other blacks (deliberately or collateral damage) don't receive his knee. In fact, they don't receive a knee, an elbow, or any limb for that matter. They don't even receive attention. Instead, they receive the finger – the middle one, figuratively speaking.

17 As shepherd of one particular flock, Knee-sus will not cast pearls (in the form of a knee) before swine. His focus is on the black sheep.

18 And any acknowledgment of the fact that black-on-black carnage routinely accounts for more than half of the United States' annual homicide tally[lvii] would weaken his narrative about the badged boogeymen.

19 A mother in Baton Rouge, LA. believed that her army veteran son was safer in an Iraqi war zone than in the urban America war zone where he was killed.[lviii] And in Kent, Washington, a mother lost her teenaged son and daughter six months apart to urban terrorism.[lix] A father in Buffalo, NY. unfathomably lost three children a few years apart — his two sons were shot dead, and daughter stabbed to death.[lx] These types of stories number in the thousands but amount to nothing in Knee-sus' ministry.

20 For further proof of Knee-sus' selectivity, look no further than his birthplace: Milwaukee, Wisconsin. He's adored in the Cream City and stands as a living exception to Jesus' statement:

"A prophet is not without honor except in his hometown and among his own relatives and in his own household." [lxi]

21 When the state legislature's Black Caucus drafted a resolution to honor several black leaders for Wisconsin's Black History Month, Knee-sus was included. However, the Republican-controlled Senate stripped his name from the resolution before unanimously passing it.[lxii] The GOP's political sleight of hand infuriated Knee-sus' zealots in Milwaukee. And that anger moved Milwaukee's city council to counter the GOP's rejection of Knee-sus by highlighting him in its *"28 Days of Black History"* project.[lxiii] The Republican lawmakers may have thwarted Knee-sus from being honored state-wide, but the Cream City's Democratic lawmakers ensured that the cream of its crop was locally honored.

22 Yet, Knee-sus' ministry doesn't reciprocate the love or sympathy to Milwaukee's murdered, non-Knee-groes. And there's an abundance of non-Knee-groes because his birthplace is routinely one of America's most dangerous cities. Furthermore, it's a place where ~~thug~~ gun violence has reached levels so epidemic that activists want it to be treated as a public health crisis.[lxiv]

> CAN WE FIGHT MILWAUKEE'S GUN VIOLENCE EPIDEMIC BY TREATING IT LIKE A PUBLIC HEALTH CRISIS?
>
> ZACH BROOKE x APRIL 27, 2018

23 This past year, Milwaukee ranked fourth on World Atlas' 2018 list of the *"25 Most Dangerous Cities in the United States,"* and tenth on USA Today's "*50 Worst Cities to Live In.*"

24 Additionally, Neighborhood Scout gave the city a crime index ranking of four (out of a hundred), which means that Milwaukee is statistically more violent than ninety-six percent of U.S. cities.

25 In the "Year of the Knee," 24/7 Wall Street listed Milwaukee as the fifth most violent city in America (with at least 100,000 people). It also noted that the number of violent crimes in Milwaukee rose by 60.5 percent between 2010 to 2015. Within only five years, Milwaukee jumped from the twenty-ninth spot on 24/7 Wall Street's list of "*Most Dangerous U.S. Cities*" to fifth. In 2017 and 2018, it was listed at eighth and seventh respectively.

26 A WisconsinWatch.org article titled, "*Bullets exacted terrible toll on children, African Americans*" stated that in 2014: "*African Americans, who make up 6.5 percent of the state's population, accounted for about two-thirds of its firearm homicide* *victims. Blacks in Wisconsin were more than 30 times as likely as non-Hispanic whites to die in gun homicides. From 2008 to 2012, federal statistics show, this ratio was 20 to 1 for Wisconsin and 10 to 1 for the nation."* [lxv]

27 In August of 2018, the Milwaukee Journal Sentinel observed: *"For the past several years, about a quarter of Milwaukee's homicides have stemmed from an argument or fight. Nearly all of those homicides involved a gun."* [lxvi]

28 Blacks are approximately thirty-nine-percent of Milwaukee's population but are disproportionately responsible for and affected by the city's violent crime.

29 Blacks, such as 6-year-old Justin Evans Jr., who was coldheartedly shot dead in his grandmother's backyard by ~~thug~~ gun violence as he prepared to leave on a fishing trip. The soon-to-be first-grader was Milwaukee's youngest victim of gun violence in 2017. His shooting occurred less than a week after two girls, ages 7 and 9, were also shot.

30 A year earlier, the death of 23-year-old Sylville Smith[lxvii] (a ~~career criminal~~ law-abiding citizen), sparked what became known as "The Milwaukee Riots." Armed with a stolen semiautomatic handgun that contained twenty-three rounds, he was shot and killed by an officer during a foot chase after fleeing a traffic stop. The ensuing collective temper-tantrum lasted three days and resulted in looting, police cars vandalized/torched, and arson attacks on several businesses.[lxviii] A fire set at a gas station burned freely for hours because gunshots in the area prevented firefighters from responding. The angry mob also threw rocks and bricks at officers, injuring four. And after the mayor's plea for peace fell on deaf ears, Wisconsin's governor activated the National Guard. The Milwaukee Riots yielded one death, multiple injuries, dozens of arrests, and millions in damages.

31 Milwaukee's urban unrest and chocolate chaos or **_"Black rage,"_** as Knee-sus calls it, only occurred on Smith's behalf because of his Knee-groe designation. As fate would

---

have it, the twenty-three bullets that Smith's stolen gun contained, ended up being representative of his years on Earth. Luckily for him, Knee-sus' flock will forever promote the way those twenty-years ended as opposed to the way they were recklessly spent.

32 Knee-sus' flock also guarantees that the world doesn't forget Knee-groes such as Sandra Bland, who was found hanged in a jail cell on July 13th, 2015 (her death ruled a suicide).lxix Whereas, non-Knee-groes such as 13-year-old Sandra Parks, who was killed on November 19th, 2018 by a stray bullet in her room, only receive a world of indifference.

33 Sandra Parks' sister described young Sandra taking the deadly bullet (which pierced her chest) *"like a soldier."* And added, *"She just walked in the room and said, 'Mama, I'm shot.'"*

34 Two years before her demise, Sandra wrote an award-winning essay as a sixth-grader titled, *"Our Truth."* Her intimate and sobering essay highlighted Milwaukee's gun violence and its effect on the young. She expressed, *"there is too much black-on-black crime,"* and described her hometown as being in *"a state of chaos."* Sandra spoke from the heart when writing, *"In a city in which I live, I hear and see examples of*

chaos almost everyday. Little children are victims of senseless gun violence." In 2018, Sandra Parks was the seventh Milwaukee public school student to be murdered.[lxx]

35 Between the years 2015 and 2018, a total of eighteen Knee-groes (three unarmed) were martyred in the state of Wisconsin.[lxxi] During that same period, Milwaukee annually averaged more than a hundred homicides after peaking at 145 in 2015.[lxxii] And though Milwaukee's non-Knee-groes will continue to outnumber Knee-groes, the former will always be treated like zeros and the latter like heroes.

Only Knee-groes are worthy of documentaries

36 And this favoritism isn't isolated to the city of Knee-sus' origin story; it's nationwide.

37 Jacksonville, Florida, which is a city that Neighborhoodscout.com has given a crime index rating of nine (a hundred is the safest), and often holds the dubious reputation as the state's murder capital,[lxxiii] experienced a traumatic eleven-day period in February 2018.

38 Within that time, five different juveniles were shot, including 7-year-old Tashawn Gallon. The first-grader was playing in a front yard when drive-by crossfire between two gangs of urban terrorists struck and killed him. Jacksonville's Mayor tweeted, *"They didn't hesitate to recklessly turn our streets into a war zone."*

39 Later that year, in August, urban terrorists shot up a high school's Friday Night Lights football game as fans departed. The gunfire was unscheduled overtime action that resulted in one death and two injuries. The troubling incident made national news. Nearly sixty officers were in attendance as deterrents, but the thugs were determined not to be deterred.

⁴⁰ Two days after that brazen Friday Night Lights shooting, the Jacksonville Jaguars (which has disciples of Knee-sus on the roster) played their third 2018 preseason football game. The city was trying to heal, and this game was an excellent opportunity for the disciples to assist with that endeavor altruistically. Showing some (pre or post-game) love to the victims and their families would've gone a long way. Instead, the disciples stayed true to Knee-sus' ministry and didn't deviate from it one jot or tittle. There was no acknowledgment of the victims as if the tragic incident never happened.

⁴¹ The blind-eye act reflected their commitment to Knee-sus. The commitment had been on display since the team's first preseason game. During the national anthem, they had flat-out remained in the locker room. No time was wasted on taking a knee, sitting, or raising a fist on the sideline. This variation of the protest gesture was new for the 2018 season. However, the same old message of unworthiness was sent to non-

Knee-groes like the high school shooting victims and 7-year-old Tashawn Gallon.

42 In Miami, Florida, a couple of Knee-sus' disciples on the Miami Dolphins' football team stuck with the traditional kneeling protest for their first 2018 preseason game, while a third disciple chose the raised fist. Never mind Miami's crime index rating of six (one hundred is the safest) from Neighborhoodscout.com, or its status as one of the worst cities for solving homicides[lxxiv] (60 percent unsolved between 2007 and 2017) — Knee-groes remain the focal point.

43 Now and then, the disciples who've faithfully adhered to Knee-sus' ministry or displayed real loyalty, are blessed with a shout-out on social media from the Knee-man himself. Such was the case for one of the aforementioned Miami disciples. He had taken a knee against *"systemic oppression"* at every NFL game since Knee-sus showed him the light. And Lo! Knee-sus shined his Twitter light on the devotee for him to bask in it.

[44] It bears repeating; Knee-sus' heart is hardened against black victims who aren't Knee-groes because Knee-groes are his ministry's lifeblood.

[45] Consequently, his mission orbits around the notion that police (not violent black criminals) are the supreme threat to black people.

[46] His detractors regularly rebuke that premise and dismiss it as a falsehood. They claim that the police are not an imminent threat to black people.

[47] And as expected, Knee-sus' disciples vehemently disagree; as does the ~~synthetic~~ grassroots group Black Lives Matter (BLM). Like Knee-sus, BLM also ~~exploits~~ advocates for this same minute group of black people (Knee-groes).

[48] He who has ears to hear, let him hear! Knee-sus and Black Lives Matter ~~are~~ aren't telling the same lies. These two ~~conniving~~ inspired entities are conductors on the same track with the same type of passengers (Knee-groes); only their trains are different.

The non-believers are hell-bent on derailing this new-age Underground Railroad.

⁴⁹ BLM's connection to Knee-sus isn't by chance; it's celestial! This organization ~~of opportunists~~ was Knee-sus' forerunner. It prepared the way for his coming just as John the Baptist did for Jesus Christ (Mark 1:2-3).

⁵⁰ The ~~revealing~~ slanderous book, *"Black Lies Matter,"* posits that BLM is a wholly-owned subsidiary of the Racial Grievance Industry (RGI). It describes the RGI as a parasitic entity that cunningly and unremittingly uses three schemes to sustain itself: black victimhood, white guilt, and political correctness.

⁵¹ The RGI knows that the black victimhood it peddles can easily be parlayed into racial vendettas, and then escalated into racial violence. Recall, Knee-sus explained that this type of racial violence is actually ***"Black-rage,"*** manifesting as ***"a beautiful form of defiance."***

⁵² For those who aren't familiar with the RGI, its members characteristically employ RGI-sanctioned math for any confliction resolution between black and white people. The math is basic and doesn't require a calculator. Though, if executed correctly, a calculator may be needed to count the accumulated funds. Here's the math:

- *Subtract* the individuality of involved parties.
- *Add* racial identities as replacements. (The involved parties must be treated as representatives of their respective races.)
- Create *division* by emphasizing racial identities. Make it about race!
- *Multiply* the support for the newly manufactured racial grievance via social media.

[53] The math always yields the same answer; black people are victims.

[54] One of the most familiar faces of today's RGI is known by many monikers. The most common are Talcum X or Martin Luther Cream (MLC). Those nicknames poke fun because he ~~allegedly~~ isn't black but plays one on social media. Regardless of what he's called, his masterful ability to engineer racial grievances can only be called one thing: legendary.

[55] MLC, whose Twitter header includes a picture of himself hugging an elated Knee-sus, brought in the year 2019 with his racial grievance guns blazing. He had just received word that on December 30th, 2018, a white man in a pickup truck pulled alongside a black 7-year-old girl and her mother as they drove from Walmart, and indiscriminately

fired shots into the vehicle. The 7-year-old girl was fatally wounded.

56 Her mother said that the shooter, who was described as a bearded white man in his 40's with a red hooded sweatshirt, *"intentionally"* killed her daughter Jasmine Barnes. From a hospital bed, she recalled the heartbreaking incident.[lxxv]

"As I turned around and looked back at the street, I heard shots start firing and they came through my window, broke my glass, and hit me in my arm. They sped off in front of us and the truck slowed down and continued to fire as he was in front of us. It was not fair. It was not fair. He intentionally killed my child for no reason. He didn't even know her, he didn't know who she was."

Sketch of the Suspect

57 Even before the alleged shooter's sketch was released, MLC had already judged the white man by the color of his skin as being a white supremacist. And in an attempt to expedite the suspect's capture, he typed *"Urgent. All Hands On Deck"* to his vast social media following (3 million followers between Twitter and Facebook). He implored them to send tips directly to him in exchange for a possible $75K reward. The reward eventually ballooned to $100K with the assistance of a prominent RGI Civil Rights attorney.[lxxvi]

58 On January 3rd, 2019, MLC wrote an article for Black America Web that was titled, *"We Need To Find The Man Who Murdered Jazmine Barnes"* He started the commentary with his belief that *"2019 is going to be a good year for us."* It's unclear if the *"us"* that he referred to meant black people or the RGI. I'm assuming that it was the latter since he ~~allegedly~~ isn't black. ‾_(ツ)_/‾

59 MLC's commentary highlighted Jazmine's shooting and his ambitious online dragnet. He wrote:

"Listen, I have some heavy news this morning, but I also have some great news. I'm going to start with the horrible murder of 7-year-old Jazmine Barnes in Houston, Texas this past weekend. As you may have already seen online, I am doing my very best to track down her killer, and have a $75,000 reward for information leading to the arrest of this middle-aged white man who pulled up in a red truck and intentionally shot Jazmine in the head, and also shot her mother, LaPorsha."

60 His massive social media hunt quickly led to a white man who fit the sketch. MLC posted the white man's picture and name along with the implication that he was Jazmine's killer. He then requested his deputized followers to provide more information about the white suspect:

"He was arrested in Houston hours after Jazmine was murdered on another violent crime spree. We've had 20 people call or email us and say he is a racist, violent asshole and always has been. Just tell me everything you know."

61 The photo of the suspected killer instantly went viral, and the suspect's family was harshly harassed and threatened. The danger of violent vigilantism to his loved ones was real. One Facebook post mentioned the possibility of women and children in his family being raped, tortured, and murdered.[lxxvii]

62 The RGI's clergy arm had also got involved in the race to capture *"America's real terrorist threat,"* as one of its Bishops tweeted:

"This is 7-year-old #JazmineBarnes. She didn't die in custody of Border Patrol. She was shot and killed by America's real terrorist threat, a white man who opened fire on her family's car as they left Walmart in

Houston. The shooter is still at large. #SayHerName."

"The mother of #JasmineBarnes, her & yr old daughter who was shot & killed by a white supremacist. The murderer pulled up in a red truck & opened fire into their car on Dec 30 in Houston. He's still at large. This is America for Black people. #SayHerName"

63 The *"SayHerName"* hashtag is a product of an RGI-based social movement that aspires to raise awareness for black female victims of police or anti-black violence.[lxxviii] In other words, it's a crusade for a minority within an already minority subset: female Knee-groes.

64 Numerous celebrities got involved with Jazmine Barnes' case. Basketball Hall-of-Famer, Shaquille O' Neal, and De'Andre Hopkins, a star receiver for the NFL's Houston Texans volunteered to pay the 7-year-old's funeral expenses. Hopkins pledged his hefty $29,000 playoff game check to her family and tweeted:

"When I see Jazmine Barnes' face, I see my own daughter. I'm pledging my playoff check

this week to help her family with funeral costs and to support @shaunking @SherriffED_HCSO @SylvesterTurner in bringing this man to justice. On Saturday, I will be playing in your honor, Jazmine."

65 All of the love and support that emanated from the black united front for Jasmine came to a screeching halt when the actual killers were apprehended. The perpetrators were two black thugs.

66 The white suspect who MLC made infamous, turned out to be an innocent bystander that fled the crime scene as the bullets flew. MLC has yet to issue a public apology to the white man or his family for seriously placing them in harm's way. History shows that an apology will likely never happen. It isn't MLC's forte to apologize; only racialize.

67 Case in point: In May of 2018, MLC used his standard racial rabble-rousing (via social media) to identify a white Dallas police officer who allegedly sexually assaulted a black woman during a suspected DUI/DWI traffic stop. When writing about the alleged rape, MLC channeled his inner Knee-sus and declared, [lxxix] *"This system was not designed to protect us — it was designed to punish us."*

68 And just like he used his social media platform to convict the white suspect in Jazmine Barnes' case, the white officer was also found guilty in MLC's kangaroo court.

69 The officer's life instantaneously became a living hell, and the police department faced immense pressure to release his body camera footage prematurely. The department summarily obliged. To MLC's chagrin, the nearly two-hour video showed the officer being completely professional to the intoxicated woman. Her accusation was an outright, head-scratching, lie. Holy Tawana Brawley!

70 In response to the hoax, MLC wrote a lengthy, backpedaling post that attempted to paint himself as the victim. His 1,335-word spiel didn't contain one apologetic word or sentence to the falsely accused officer.[lxxx]

71 It was par for the course. The racial grievance rodeos that MLC creates come with no apologies or refunds.

72 And now that Jazmine Barnes' demise lacked a racial component, she was no longer a cause célèbre. MLC went back to his lair, the "concerned" celebrities tip-toed back to their Ivory towers, the Kente-Kamikaze fell silent on social media, and nobody demanded accountability from the source of the lie.[lxxxi]

73 The RGI had effectively revoked Jazmine Barnes' platinum status and treated the deceased 7-year-old as a persona non grata.

74 In Memphis, Tenn., 2-year-old Laylah Washington had also been categorized as a persona non grata. Her and Jazmine Barnes' stories are eerily similar. Actually, the manner of their deaths is similar. The reactions to their deaths were outstandingly different.

[75] In June of 2017, 2-year-old Laylah was riding in a car with her mother from a Dollar General store when two black thugs pulled alongside them and repeatedly fired into the vehicle. Like Jasmine, Laylah was fatally injured.

[76] Although Laylah's story captivated the city of Memphis, the shooters remained on the loose. And because the shooters were the usual suspects (black thugs), the RGI's first responders showed no interest with assisting in their capture. Moreover, no black professional athlete in Memphis came forward to reflect about Laylah being a reminder of their daughter as DeAndre Hopkins had done with Jazmine Barnes. However, two months after Laylah's death (and with her killers still at large), the basketball coach for the Memphis Grizzlies did come forward to say that he'd kneel with his team for Knee-sus' mission if the players ever decided to kneel.

By | September 25, 2017 at 9:50 PM CDT - Updated August 16 at 2:57 AM

77 Unlike Jasmine's situation where a $100K reward was rapidly raised to find the perpetrators, the Memphis Police had to resort to offering a $20K reward (almost a year after Laylah's death) to stimulate more tips.

78 And it took nearly a year and a half (Christmas 2018) for the two urban terrorists to be arrested and charged. Their capture occurred a week before Jasmine's untimely death.

2 charged in fatal shooting of Tennessee toddler

Memphis police say two men have been arrested the killing of a 2-year-old girl who was shot while riding in a car with her mother.

Wednesday, December 26th 2018, 8:01 AM EST

79 The pitchforks strikingly came out for Jasmine Barnes, but only pitch silence emerged for Laylah Washington. There was no comparably aggressive social media pursuit or tips; even if those tips would've incriminated the wrong person who happened to be right for the RGI's agenda.

[80] This is the situation whenever the offender is a brotherman and not the badged boogeyman. Thus, don't be upset with Knee-sus for playing by the same rules as the RGI. Cherry-picking black people's deaths while ignoring the fields of black bodies delivered by black hands is a time-honored tradition that existed long before his coming.

CLICK▶ON
DETROIT

3-year-old boy dies after being shot on Southfield Freeway on Detroit's west side

Child's godmother was taking him to see Sesame Street Live play, police say

PRIYA MANN, DERICK HUTCHINSON
JANUARY 25, 2019 5:22 PM

On January 24th, 2019, 3-year-old Christian "CJ" Miller was riding with his Godmother to see Sesame St. Live in Detroit when a black thug pulled alongside them and fired shots. Little CJ was killed while sitting in his car seat. Question: Did CJ's death receive the Laylah Washington treatment... or the Jazmine Barnes treatment? It's a rhetorical question :/

[81] You must comprehend that Knee-sus didn't come to change the game of victimhood; he came to fulfill it.

CHAPTER III

Cruci-Fiction

1 Despite the perceived hypocrisy of Knee-sus' ministry and the controversy it created for the NFL during the "Year of the Knee," his popularity had surpassed any achievement gained as an unreliable quarterback.

2 Going primetime from the sideline became a self-fulling prophesy.

3 Flashback to the 2015 season, when he initially began shuffling between the starter and backup roles. At that time, his jersey and related merchandise were heavily discounted to basement prices on the team's online store.[lxxxii] This type of scorched-earth markdown usually indicates an ending relationship between a team and a player.

4 Undeniably, Knee-sus' future with the team appeared bleak.

5 But, behold! A mere season later (the Year of the Knee), his jersey sales were through the roof!

6 CBS Sports reported that three of the top six jerseys sold on his team's website were specifically related to him. And one particular week experienced more Knee-sus paraphernalia being purchased than the past eight months combined! To Knee-sus be the glory!

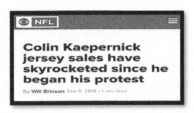

Colin Kaepernick jersey sales have skyrocketed since he began his protest

By Will Brinson Sep 5, 2016 · 1 min read

[7] Lo! The spike in jersey sales wasn't confined to his team's online store; the NFL's online store had likewise felt the power of the knee. His jersey became the top-seller on the site and supplanted many notable Super Bowl-winning quarterbacks such as Russell Wilson and Tom Brady.

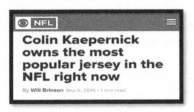

Colin Kaepernick owns the most popular jersey in the NFL right now

By Will Brinson Sep 6, 2016 · 1 min read

[8] Knee-sus' ~~ploy~~ revelation was paying supreme dividends. His meteoric rise (by sitting) was comparable to Bitcoin's meteoric rise that also happened by sitting. Both Knee-sus and Bitcoin's actions were unanticipated, swift, and game-changing.

[9] Yet, neither could avoid Sir Isaac Newton's axiom of physics; *"What goes up, must come down."* Their spectacular ascensions were destined for spectacular descensions.

[10] Typically, a controversial figure is revered by some, villainized by others, or viewed ambivalently by everyone else.

[11] Unfortunately for Knee-sus, there was no middle. People either perceived him as a hero or villain.

[12] For that reason, it wasn't paradoxical for him to own the NFL's top-selling jersey while also owning the top vote as the NFL's most disliked player.

[13] In God Goodell's eyes, Knee-sus was a fallen angel causing mayhem.

[14] Knee-sus had dared to be a controversial being, and God Goodell (who is a jealous God) doesn't want controversy from his angels; he wants conformity. Non-conformists most certainly risk banishment from his NFL garden.

15 Knee-sus' former fans, many of whom burned his jersey, believed that he only showed up on Sundays to spread his ministry. Fulfillment of his contractual obligations as a quarterback was secondary.

16 This perception became part of Knee-sus' new normal; all because he single-handedly repurposed NFL games.

17 I submit this humble observation; Sunday belonged to the church long before the NFL commandeered it. Therefore, Knee-sus was merely reclaiming Sunday for the church, his church — the Church of the Eternal Victim. (REFER TO CHAPTER 5)

18 He clairvoyantly understood that this battle with God Goodell would be difficult and potentially career-ending. Still, Knee-sus was willing to be crucified for his beliefs. He proclaimed: [lxxxiii]

"If they take football away, my endorsements from me, I know that I stood up for what is right."

19 The "they" that Knee-sus alluded to were God Goodell, media, NFL sponsors, moneychangers (gamblers), non-believers, and NFL's Pharisees (NFL team owners). Many of whom had hoped for his precipitous downfall in one way or another.

20 Supreme Court Justice, Ruth Bader Ginsburg, called Knee-sus' protest *"dumb and disrespectful"* and equated it to a flag burning.[lxxxiv]

21 Several of his prominent NFL peers, including retired ones, joined the choir of public condemnation without hesitation. They'd rather be irritated by athlete's feet (the fungal infection) than by athletes who wouldn't stand on their feet for the national anthem.

22 Boomer Esiason, a former quarterback, turned NFL analyst, said that he was disgusted by Knee-sus. To him, Knee-sus was a *"complete and utter distraction and a disgrace."* He added that the kneeling was *"one of the most disgraceful displays I've ever seen by a professional athlete on his field of play."* As a remedy, Esiason recommended that Knee-sus be cut from the team.[lxxxv]

23 Mike Ditka, a Hall of Famer and Super Bowl-winning coach, said that he *"had no respect"* for Knee-sus. He also called the protest a problem, and suggested that people who disrespect America and the flag *"get the hell out."* [lxxxvi]

24 Drew Brees, an All-Pro, Super Bowl-winning quarterback for the New Orleans Saints and future Hall of Famer, expressed that he had wholeheartedly disagreed with Knee-sus' manner of protest and *"felt compelled to speak out."* Brees elaborated:

"[T]here's plenty of other ways that you can do that in a peaceful manner that doesn't involve being disrespectful to the American flag." [lxxxvii]

25 Victor Cruz, an All-Pro receiver for the New York Giants, wanted Knee-sus to know:

"You've got to respect the flag and stand up with your teammates. It's bigger than just you, in my opinion." [lxxxviii]

26 Cruz's teammate, Giants' offensive lineman Justin Pugh, tweeted his slight to Knee-sus:

"I will be STANDING during the National Anthem tonight. Thank you to ALL (Gender, Race, Religion) that put your lives on the line for that flag." [lxxxix]

27 Perhaps, the most famous rebuke from Knee-sus' peers came from Rodney Harrison, a two-time Super Bowl champion, and current football analyst. Not only did Harrison state that Knee-sus *"sitting his butt down"* wasn't going to change anything, Harrison fixed his mouth to say that Knee-sus didn't understand what black people face because *"he's* (Knee-sus) *not black."* Harrison was adamant. *"I tell you this, I'm a* *black man. And Colin Kaepernick — he's not black."*

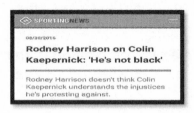

28 His statement was unadulterated blasphemy! How dare he question Knee-sus' ethnicity? Harrison realized as much and later apologized for his forked tongue. He claimed to have been unaware of Knee-sus' racial identity.

29 What fools these mortals be! Knee-sus is black, even though he has a white mother and black father. The racial dynamic of his parents is the same as former President Obama, whom everyone knows is black, right?

30 Behold! Knee-sus and Obama's shared ethnicity is not the only commonality between these two saviors. Knee-sus' black birth father bailed on the family just as President Obama's black birth father did.

31 Is more proof of Knee-sus' blackness needed? His hairstyles of choice are cornrows and afros! This preference is definitely a black thing!

³² Everything about Knee-sus reflects blackness! Well, everything except for his comfortable upbringing by adoptive white parents in a whitopia (white-topia). Oh, and his girlfriend, Messy Magdalene. But, that's beside the point.

³³ And because Knee-sus and President Obama are brothers from another mother, Obama felt comfortable with giving Knee-sus a respectful piece of advice.

³⁴ From one savior to another, he wanted Knee-sus and the kneelers to think about the emotional discomfort they may cause military families whenever they took a knee. Obama advised:

"I want them to listen to the pain that that may cause somebody who, for example, had a spouse or a child who was killed in combat, and why it hurts them to see somebody not standing." [xc]

³⁵ Obama's advice went unanswered. Knee-sus trooped onward to spread his gospel, his way. But danger loomed; danger far more threatening than the constant criticisms.

³⁶ Knee-sus had received death threats.

³⁷ Being half-black, half-white, half-quarterback, and half social justice warrior, Knee-sus knew how to navigate a dual existence. However, navigating a dual

existence between life and death was unchartered terrain. It was an X-factor in his divine plan.

38 For that reason, he had to address this pressing issue for the mission's sake. So, Knee-sus courageously put on his game face (the one that he wore on NFL sidelines) and communicated:

"[I]f something like that were to happen, you've proved my point and it will be loud and clear for everyone why it happened, and that would move this movement forward at a greater speed than what it is even now." [xci]

39 Knee-sus' response to the threat of death was reminiscent of something Obi-Wan Kenobi had stated to Darth Vader in Star Wars IV. During a lightsaber duel, Obi-Wan warned Darth Vader, *"If you strike me down, I shall become more powerful than you can possibly imagine."*

40 Knee-sus' words were proof that the force was with him. Agents of the dark side that wished to inflict harm were cautioned. Still, he was genuinely concerned that a weapon formed against him might prosper.

41 He further preached about the death threats and clarified his feelings:

"Granted, it's not how I want it to happen, but that's the realization of what could happen. I knew there were other things that came along with this when I first stood up and spoke about it. It's not something I haven't thought about."

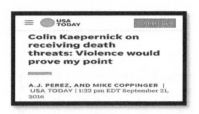

42 Here's the reality. Everybody wants to go to heaven, but nobody wants to die to get there. Knee-sus is no exception.

43 Speaking of heaven, God Goodell desperately wanted the league's ratings to return to their heavenly status enjoyed before the Year of the Knee.

44 Kneeling had become bad optics for the NFL and was a primary reason for the league's ratings plunge. Forbes.com observed:

"[D]isrespecting the country during the national anthem is accomplishing what the concussions, domestic violence and deflategate could not do--drive down television ratings for the National Football League." [xcii]

45 Knee-sus was unremorseful about the NFL's so-called bad optics, and for a good reason. His impact was raining steadily on the league like manna from heaven.

46 But God Goodell was livid. The multibillion-dollar league that he ruled with an iron fist was slipping from his grasp in real time.

47 The most popular professional sports league in the United States that he was ordained to fashion for the financial benefit of the NFL's Pharisees had become unrecognizable.

48 Although there's no rule in the NFL that requires players to stand during the national anthem (God Goodell prefers that players stand), God Goodell disagreed with the protests, but reluctantly tolerated the players' ability to do so. He went on record to say:

"We believe very strongly in patriotism in the NFL. I think it's important to have respect for our country, for our flag, for the people who make our country better; for law enforcement, and for our military who are out fighting for our freedoms and our ideals."

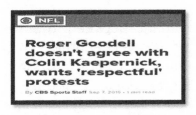

Roger Goodell doesn't agree with Colin Kaepernick, wants 'respectful' protests
By CBS Sports Staff Sep 7, 2016 · 1 min read

[49] The NFL Players' Union (NFLPA) often clashes with God Goodell. He believes that its members are mostly disagreeable angels who speak his name in vain. The feeling is mutual. This is why God Goodell's non-support for Knee-sus' mission meant the NFLPA's automatic support for Knee-sus' mission.

[50] The NFLPA considers itself the only family that NFL players have outside of their actual families. And since Knee-sus was not the begotten son of God Goodell, the NFLPA felt that God Goodell shouldn't treat him as such.

[51] The head of the NFLPA even let it be known that expecting athletes to "shut up

and play" isn't respecting them as fully human — even though Knee-sus isn't fully human.[xciii]

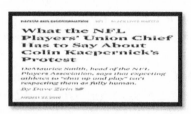

52 This covenant between the NFLPA and Knee-sus posed yet another challenge (a public relations challenge) to God Goodell. He was in a precarious situation.

53 On the one hand, he didn't want to appear insensitive to Knee-sus' mission, but on the other hand, he had to appease the NFL's Pharisees, and NFL's patriotic fan base.

54 The founder and CEO of Papa John's pizza, which was a sponsor of the NFL, would later have harsh words for God Goodell. From the onset of the rebellion, he wanted God Goodell to impose his will onto the players and force them to stand during the National Anthem. The CEO barked:

"We are disappointed the NFL and its leadership did not resolve this. Leadership starts at the top and this is an example of poor leadership." [xciv]

[55] The owner of the Washington Redskins complained that real business issues were at stake, especially in his Washington, D.C. market, where the defense industry and other sponsors were angry about the protests.[xcv]

[56] In a league that is nearly seventy-percent black, the late-owner of the Houston Texans had a warden-like response to the protesting: *"We can't have the inmates running the prison."* He would later express regret for the ill-advised analogy.[xcvi]

[57] One NFL executive expressed (about Knee-sus) that *"he hasn't seen this much collective dislike among front office members regarding a player since Rae Carruth."*[xcvii] For the record, Rae Carruth is a former Carolina Panthers wide receiver and convicted felon who had his pregnant girlfriend shot dead to avoid paying child support.[xcviii] Now, let that Knee-sus/Carruth correlation marinate.

[58] Though that comparison to Rae Carruth was a barometer of the abhorrence for Knee-sus at the NFL executive-level, it stayed in-house. God Goodell was in dire need of an independent, influential voice that could call-out Knee-sus with impunity, and articulate the true feelings of himself, the NFL's Pharisees, sponsors, and patriotic fan base.

⁵⁹ As fate would have it, one such powerful voice appeared. And it came in the personage of Orange Herod, a ~~wickedly outspoken~~ wicked Republican politician who was running for President of the United States.

⁶⁰ Knee-sus' knee-atrics had made Orange Herod red with anger. So, Orange Herod embarked on a mission to make football great again.

⁶¹ His view of Knee-sus as an unappreciative, overpaid, and entitled athlete quickly made him Knee-sus' main archnemesis.

⁶² Whenever the opportunity presented itself, even if on the campaign trail, Orange Herod wouldn't hesitate to scold him publicly. He once recommended that Knee-sus *"find a country that works better for him."* And then doubled-down on the recommendation by guaranteeing that *"it's not gonna happen."* ˣᶜⁱˣ

⁶³ Orange Herod would eventually become President, and from the bully pulpit, his heckling intensified. The relentless jeering wasn't limited to Knee-sus; players that followed Knee-sus were also demonized.

⁶⁴ President Orange Herod once encouraged fans to the leave stadiums if they see players kneeling just as the Vice President

did at an Indianapolis Colts/San Francisco 49ers game.

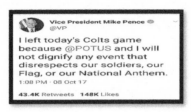

65 On another occasion, he asked:

"Wouldn't you love to see one of these NFL owners, when somebody disrespects our flag, to say, 'Get that son of a bitch off the field right now. Out! He's fired. He's fired!'"

66 The Sunday that followed his inflammatory *"son of a bitch"* comment, approximately two-hundred players knelt or locked arms in solidarity and defiance during the National Anthem.[c] Knee-sus Nation had sent a strong and visible message to President Orange Herod.

67 His successful ascension to the Oval Office as a non-politician had surprised many people; particularly his popular, female, Democratic opponent who had staunchly defended the NFL players' right to be like Knee-sus.

68 She was a career politician with the presidency on her political bucket list. Her campaign slogan was *"I'm with her,"* and rest assured, her large black electorate was definitely "with her." She once bragged about carrying hot sauce in her bag as a nod to her black base.[ci]

69 Oddly, Knee-sus was not *"with her."* He didn't support her candidacy, even though she supported his mission and virtue-signaled to black folk. ~~like he did.~~

70 In fact, after watching the presidential debate between the two candidates (which he called embarrassing), Knee-sus determined that both candidates were: *"[P]roven liars,"* who ***"almost seems like they're trying to debate who's less racist."***

71 His overall assessment of the presidential debate was this:

"[A]t this point ... you have to pick the lesser of two evils. But in the end, it's still evil."

72 In the end, Knee-sus didn't vote in the 2016 Presidential election. He believed that his vote was best utilized by leaving it on the bench.

73 His decision to refrain from voting drew side-eyes from many allies. The political Left had deployed all resources to ensure that Orange Herod didn't become president. Yet Knee-sus, who was supported by the political Left and its media, had used his influential platform to scold the Democratic Party's nominee. He even insinuated that she should be imprisoned for deleting classified emails from her private email server.[cii]

74 Ironically, Knee-sus' sentiment about her being jailed was one that Orange Herod also promoted. The phrase *"Lock Her Up"* was a staple at his campaign stops. Orange Herod's enthusiastic supporters would ceremoniously chant the catchphrase, which even made its way to the floor of the 2016 Republican National Convention.[ciii]

75 Because Knee-sus had unintentionally aligned himself with Orange Herod's *"Lock her up"* sentiment, combined with his non-vote (which critics viewed as a de facto vote for Orange Herod), several supporters on the political Left and mainstream media reined in their support for him.

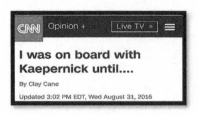

76 Thus, when the NFL's tumultuous 2016 season ended, it didn't end for Knee-sus. The good, bad, and ugliness that occurred in the Year of the Knee would unshakably follow him.

77 This reality became apparent after he opted out of his contract to become a free agent for 2017. The team expressed that Knee-sus would've been cut anyway had he not walked ~~on water~~ away.

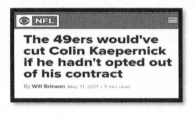

78 With his underused talent and public mission, he was certain that an exodus to the free market would generate numbers. Doors were expected to slam open from quarterback-needy teams.

79 But, his reputation as a potential distraction with a diminished skillset had preceded him. As a result, offers were slow to materialize, even from quarterback-needy teams.

80 A personnel executive from a quarterback-needy team once confessed:

"I wouldn't touch the guy. He still has some in the tank, but is not worth bringing him into your building . . . too much of a distraction and also not what you want in the locker room." [civ]

81 The New York Giants owner gave a glimpse of the responses he heard from Giants fans regarding any possible Knee-sus hiring. He said:

"All my years in the league, I never received more emotional mail from people than I did about that issue. 'If any of your players ever do that, we are never coming to another Giants game.' It wasn't one or two letters. It was a lot. It's an emotional, emotional issue for a lot of people, more so than any other issue I've run into." [cv]

82 Of course, President Orange Herod was elated about Knee-sus' circumstance. Even though the unemployment rate for black people had reached a record low during his term,[cvi] he was particularly thrilled about Knee-sus' unemployment. He even took credit for it! President Orange Herod believed that the NFL's Pharisees didn't sign Knee-sus because they feared receiving a nasty tweet from the Oval Office.[cvii]

83 Undeterred, Knee-sus felt confident that his unemployment status was temporary. No other free agent was bringing what he brought to the table. He offered a two for one deal: on-field abilities and sideline ministry. It was the best package the 2017 offseason could have hoped to receive.

84 His offering sounded like a win-win proposition, but the potential takers were taking their time to reach out to him.

85 Upon seeing this reality, Knee-sus' followers became rabidly irate. A #NoKaepernickNoNFL petition was started and accumulated thousands of signatures.[cviii] The devotees wanted God Goodell to act affirmatively on Knee-sus' behalf.

86 Sensing that this moment was ~~exploitable~~ teachable, the RGI hastily got involved to ~~racialize~~ organize on Knee-sus' behalf. A *"United We Stand"* rally (promoted by Spike Lee)[cix] was held in front of the NFL's New York City headquarters with the demand that Knee-sus get signed by the start of the 2017 regular season. More than a thousand supporters were in attendance, and many wore Knee-sus' #7 jersey. The RGI intended to unwrap one of its single-most reliable gifts: white ~~guilt~~ compassion. It's the gift that keeps giving.

They claimed to care but didn't care to spell his last name correctly???

[87] One of the greatest ~~lies~~ lines from the rally came from a Baltimore megachurch's reverend who's also an RGI majority stockholder. He preached: [cx]

"The NFL has proven with their treatment of Colin Kaepernick that they do not mind if black players get a concussion. They just got a problem if black players get a conscience."

[88] Knee-sus most certainly had a conscience. And his conscience made him conscious of the fact that being unsigned was the sign of the times.

[89] Although the rally didn't help change his employment status, Knee-sus, to his credit, maintained the patience of Job while being without a job.

[90] Sure, a few teams such as the Seattle Seahawks expressed interest, but not enough interest to start a relationship with him. The Seahawks stopped returning his calls and canceled the workouts because he

wouldn't agree to stop kneeling.[cxi] Knee-sus was definitely in the friend zone, which is really the unfriend zone.

91 But behold! In late July and early August 2017, one team was feeling risqué and seemingly desired to take things to the next level with him. That naughty team was the Baltimore Ravens. They had swiped right on his profile.

92 On the surface, the pairing seemed like an excellent fit because the Baltimore Ravens had taken chances on controversial players in the past. Also, the team had Super Bowl pedigree. They defeated Knee-sus' team in the 2012 Super Bowl.

93 The two parties had direct conversations in the DMs (direct messages), and the courtship was progressing towards a commitment. Ray Lewis, a Hall of Fame ex-linebacker for the Baltimore Ravens, played a critical role in the team's decision to court Knee-sus. Lewis revealed that the team's owner was making plans to sign the free agent quarterback.

[94] Be that as it may, here's the funny thing about plans, *"They're made to be ruined,"* as the saying goes.

[95] And ruined is precisely what happened to the plan to sign Knee-sus. It was ruined by the click of a mouse. The finger that clicked the mouse belonged to Knee-sus' girlfriend, Messy Magdalene. By not minding her business, Messy Magdalene had made a mess of things.

[96] Apparently, she never liked Ray Lewis' involvement in the talks because Lewis didn't support Knee-sus' protesting. He only supported Knee-sus' quarterbacking. Messy Magdalene viewed Ray Lewis' conditional backing as a problem. She wanted an "all or nothing" backing for her boo-thang Knee-sus.

[97] This anger triggered Messy Magdalene to visually express her true feelings about Ray Lewis via social media. On August 3rd, 2017, she posted a picture (from the movie "Django Unchained") that compared Lewis' embrace of the Baltimore Ravens owner to a slave's embrace of a white plantation owner. Messy Magdalene was indisputably calling Ray Lewis a racial sellout. A couple of days earlier, she called Ray Lewis a coward on Twitter:

"We know exactly who you are @raylewis #coward who got off a murder trial bc you had money and fame. Smells like #oj ☺"

98 Pictures are said to be worth a thousand words, but her pictures turned out to be worth two words: deal breaker.

99 The offensive imagery was the deal breaker on an already fragile situation. Ray Lewis quoted the owner's response to Messy Magdalene's posting:

"How can you crucify Ray Lewis when Ray Lewis is the one calling for Colin Kaepernick."

abc NEWS

Ray Lewis said Ravens would have signed Colin Kaepernick if not for girlfriend's tweet

By
Sep 5, 2017, 11:54 PM ET

100 For Knee-sus, 2017's open market had now become a closed market. There was a virtual "Buyer Beware" sign hovering above him. No interested team was going to tolerate Knee-sus' unhinged girlfriend on top of his already provocative reputation and ministry.

101 Still, it was the darndest thing for Knee-sus to see players with less talent, and others with no pedigree, receive quarterback jobs while he couldn't even secure a backup role.

102 Knee-sus became awash with emotion because he knew that he wasn't washed-up. He began to believe that his lack of employment wasn't due to lack of skills. Yes, he was a limited passer who struggled with accuracy and situational awareness, but the repeated brushoffs from teams who alternatively hired scrubs were suspicious.

103 The only tangible reason for team's ghosting him had to be due to his renowned sideline pastime that purportedly divided locker rooms and alienated fanbases.

104 He was a fly in the NFL's ointment and thus, blackballed to serve as a cautionary tale. And the longer he stayed unemployed, the stronger his conspiracy theory grew. It eventually grew higher than his afro.

105 John Harbaugh, the Super Bowl-winning coach of the Baltimore Ravens, scoffed at the notion of Knee-sus being "blackballed." He said the situation is more complicated

and called the term *"generic, stupid"* and *"intellectual laziness."* [cxii]

106 Michael Vick, a former All-Pro quarterback, and person who definitely knows a thing or two about being ostracized by the NFL, also vehemently disagreed with Knee-sus' conspiracy theory. Vick echoed the sentiment of Joe Montana, the 49ers' Hall-of-Fame quarterback, and four-time Super Bowl winner, who said that Knee-sus' lack of employment was due to his play, not protest.

107 Vick said, *"It has nothing to do with him being blackballed. The gesture that he made last year when he took the stand to do what he did, listen, we all appreciated it, we respected it, and it was a good thing. I really think the stand that he took has nothing to do with him not having a job playing in the National Football League right now. And being frank, Colin didn't have the best two years his last two seasons. It wasn't as productive as what we've seen him do."* [cxiii]

108 Not only did Vick dispute Knee-sus' conspiracy theory, but he also gave Knee-sus unsolicited advice to increase his chances of being signed. He proposed that Knee-sus cut his afro and rebuild his image. Vick counseled:

"I'm not up here to try to be politically correct but even if he puts it in cornrows, I don't think he should represent himself in that way, in terms of the hairstyle. Just go clean cut. Why not? You're already dealing with a lot, a lot of controversy surrounding this issue. The thing that he needs to do is just try to be presentable." [cxiv]

109 Vick's shocking suggestion that Knee-sus cut his hair was tantamount to Delilah suggesting Samson do the same. If Knee-sus cut his hair, he'd be cutting his ~~public relations~~ cultural identity.

110 However, in October 2017, news traveled around the NFL that Knee-sus had offered to sacrifice something profoundly more personal than his hair.

111 He offered his sacred knee. 😱

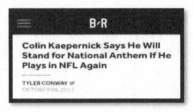

[112] Many sources, including ESPN, reported that Knee-sus was willing to abdicate his protest, if necessary, to obtain an NFL job.[cxv]

[113] Naturally, his followers were stunned and in disbelief. Some of them wondered if Knee-sus, the martyr for their movement, had actually compromised himself to become a martyr for the money. Others mused about Knee-sus possibly being a... (wait for it) fraud.

[114] Once again, Messy Magdalene powered up her social media platform. This time, it was with the sole intent to set the record straight. She tweeted:

"The reports that Colin will stand for the anthem are completely false! He has never discussed this with anyone."

NESSA
@nessnitty

The reports that Colin will stand for the anthem are completely false! He has never discussed this with anyone.
pic.twitter.com/tWusUBJMeF
♡ 4,157   1:43 PM · Oct 8, 2017

¹¹⁵ Knee-sus himself followed-up Messy Magdalene's tweet to end the speculation. He tweeted a popular quote:

"A lie gets halfway around the world before the truth has a chance to get its pants on."

¹¹⁶ Though he falsely attributed that quote to Winston Churchill,^{cxvi} the point was clear. Knee-sus didn't sellout to cash in. A fraud, he was not! The report turned out to be fake news.

¹¹⁷ CBS clarified that Knee-sus never said he'd stand for the National Anthem if given a chance to play.

¹¹⁸ The faithful were relieved and re-energized. All praises to Knee-sus! The wily ol' serpent's deceptive plan had failed!

---

[119] Still, Knee-sus remained deeply troubled and distressed. He firmly believed more than ever that God Goodell had forsaken him and was conspiring with the NFL's Pharisees to rain fire and brimstone down on his career.

[120] He realized that the only course of action to remove this cup of suffering was to file a grievance against them for collusion.

[121] And file, he did. The filing alleged that God Goodell and the NFL's Pharisees:

"colluded to deprive Mr. Kaepernick of employment rights in retaliation for Mr. Kaepernick's leadership and advocacy for equality and social justice and his bringing awareness to peculiar institutions still undermining racial equality in the United States." [cxvii]

[122] God Goodell categorically denied that there was collusion to blackball Knee-sus, [cxviii] but maintained his stance that NFL fans don't come to stadiums *"to be protested to."*

[123] When filing, Knee-sus deliberately did not utilize the services of the NFLPA, even though the group had earlier shown allegiance to him. The group even gave Knee-sus its Week 1 Community MVP award, despite him not being on an NFL team. [cxix]

[124] Knee-sus independently hired a lawyer for stars since he was a star. This lawyer had

represented high-profile celebrities such as singers Michael Jackson, Chris Brown, and NASCAR driver Jeremy Mayfield.

125 The NFLPA had unwittingly fallen out of Knee-sus' favor after it aligned with a rogue splinter group that was headed by one of Knee-sus' ex-disciples. Knee-sus no longer viewed the NFLPA as his advocate but the devil's advocate.

126 This splinter group, called the Players Coalition (no apostrophe), was led by Judas Jenkins. He was an All-Pro player and one of the earliest disciples to join Knee-sus' sideline crusade.

127 And like Knee-sus, he made a verbal commitment to continuous sideline protests, even if his team's owner forbade it.[cxx]

128 Judas Jenkins was a social justice warrior in his own right, so his sideline partnership with Knee-sus was inevitable. However, "partnership" was the keyword to Judas Jenkins because he was his own man.

129 His independence was even displayed through his protest gesture. He stood with a raised fist and not the classic Knee-sus kneel.

130 Although Judas Jenkins was an ally of Knee-sus, he ultimately wanted to use the sideline platform to highlight other social justice issues that were important to him but not necessarily significant to Knee-sus. Issues related to criminal justice reform such as passing clean-slate legislation and ending the money-bail system were his passions.

131 To be clear, his agenda wasn't a rebuke of Knee-sus' ministry, only an expansion to make the ministry more inclusive.

132 But unlike Knee-sus, who frequently spoke his sound-bite sermons, thoughts, and comments through social-media posts or third-party leaks, Judas Jenkins primarily talked to people in real life; especially to those who were in a position to help.

133 He made himself available to reporters, critics, apostates, and supporters. He didn't put a juke move on the responsibilities that came with being a revolutionary.

134 Judas Jenkins is on record doing ride-alongs with police, speaking with grass-roots organizers, policy advocates, legislators on Capitol Hill, and even wrote an opinion-editorial in The Washington ~~Compost~~ Post. His op-ed explained that ending racism in the criminal justice system requires much more than taking a knee.[cxxi] The Washington Post would later call him "*the new face of NFL protests*" after presuming that the original face (Knee-sus) was dead.

[135] His proactive approach to criminal justice reform propelled him to develop the Players Coalition. This group, which he started with a handful of NFL players, grew to dozens of members.

[136] Knee-sus wasn't one of them. Judas Jenkins had reportedly tried several times to bring him into the newly formed group, but Knee-sus declined.

[137] Subsequently, the Players Coalition proceeded to make meaningful moves without Knee-sus. The group sent a 10-page memo to God Goodell asking for tangible support for its social justice agenda; an agenda that aimed at transitioning from the protest phase into the progress phase through community-based programs.[cxxii]

[138] God Goodell listened to the ideas, and as recommended by the memo's "Listen & Learn Tour," went to Philadelphia to engage with leaders of community-based programs.

[139] The Players Coalition was ecstatic about God Goodell's visit. They had accomplished something that even Knee-sus did not.

Jenkins verbalized, *"Me personally, I really want to get this conversation to move away from the anthem. I think it has served its purpose."* cxxiii

140 One of the Players Coalition's members explained that he supported Judas Jenkins because Knee-sus' mission wasn't...

"really organized and communicating with nobody. Jenkins was one of those who had a better plan than what was going on. He had got the guys and officials to work with him on so many things, and that's what we're going with." cxxiv

141 Lo! The reason why Knee-sus' movement lacked a solution-based plan is that it didn't need one! Knee-sus is the light of the sports world, a star, unlike those "Johnny Come-lately" Players Coalition members! His enormous social media following and celebrity friends are a validation of his godly status. Thus, he didn't have to organize or communicate as the Players Coalition did. Knee-sus is the way, the truth, the life, and no one can be the center of attention except through him.

142 Even though the two movements had different objectives (Knee-sus wanted to dictate terms to God Goodell whereas Judas Jenkins compromised), Knee-sus gave the Players Coalition his blessing anyway. It was a public relations chess move. His true feeling was that whoever was not with him was against him, and whoever does not gather with him scatters.

143 Knee-sus' favorite disciple, Rowdy Reid, knew that his leader's blessing to the Players Coalition was artificial. Reid wanted Judas Jenkins to be publicly cursed as a co-opter of Knee-sus' movement.

144 Rowdy Reid was Knee-sus' teammate and the first player to kneel with him during the Year of the Knee. He also followed Knee-sus' knee-print and filed a collusion lawsuit against God Goodell and the NFL's Pharisees after going unsigned following the 2017 season.[cxxv] His commitment to Knee-sus was equivalent to the Apostle Peter's commitment to Jesus. Peter declared to Jesus, *"Even if I must die with you, I will not deny you!"* [cxxvi]

145 Rowdy Reid knew that his NFL career could die with Knee-sus, yet, he didn't deny Knee-sus. In fact, when Rowdy Reid was signed by the Carolina Panthers for the 2018 season, he wore Knee-sus inspired cleats and didn't deny Knee-sus. And when he defied mathematical odds by being hit with seven "random" drug tests within eleven weeks in 2018, he didn't deny Knee-sus.

[146] The NFL's drug-testing computer system randomly chooses ten players on each team for weekly screenings. There were seventy-two eligible players on Rowdy Reid's team. Yahoo Sports reported that he had just a 0.17 percent or a 1-in-588 chance of being selected that often over that amount of time given the NFL's testing guidelines.[cxxvii]

[147] In other words, he would *"have a better chance at correctly guessing a coin flip nine times in a row,"* according to Yahoo Sports. So, was it pure chance that the number of Rowdy Reid's drug tests totaled Knee-sus' jersey number (seven)? Or, were the repeated tests a message from God Goodell?

FOR THE W!N ≡

Eric Reid was hit with his 7th 'random' drug test after wearing Kaepernick cleats

By **Andrew Joseph** | *December 18, 2018 11:41 am*

[148] Either way, Rowdy Reid stay devoted. And because of his devoutness, Knee-sus loved him more than he loved any other disciple.

[149] Discipline is the root of a disciple, and this is why Rowdy Reid believed that Knee-sus (not the Players Coalition) should lead

any talks with God Goodell and the NFL's Pharisees. After all, it was Knee-sus' revelation that sparked everything.

150 Rowdy Reid also wanted the Players Coalition to wear black *"#IMWITHKAP"* T-shirts during any meetings with the NFL's brass.[cxxviii] Only through Knee-sus should all things be possible, he thought.

151 Meanwhile, the Players Coalition continued to do the improbable without Knee-sus. They established a partnership with God Goodell and the NFL's Pharisees for their social justice initiatives. The partnership agreed to dedicate close to ninety-million dollars to the Players Coalition's designated social justice programs.[cxxix] This amount was ninety times the amount that Knee-sus pledged to his chosen charities.[cxxx]

152 The collaboration was a celebratory achievement for all involved parties and beneficiaries: The Players Coalition, God Goodell, NFL's Pharisees, and most importantly, community programs.

153 On the flip side, *"The partnership was not celebrated by everyone,"* wrote theundefeated.com.

"Kaepernick supporters in particular accused coalition members of selling out and taking

"hush money," particularly when Jenkins announced the following day that he would no longer raise his fist in protest." [cxxxi]

154 Rowdy Reid called the league's contribution a *"charade,"* and accused the Players Coalition of meeting with God Goodell and the NFL's Pharisees behind Knee-sus' back.

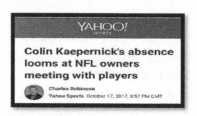

155 Jenkins denied the accusation and responded that his coalition had asked Knee-sus to attend the meeting, but he declined.

156 Knee-sus begged to differ,[cxxxii] and then sicced his high-priced lawyer on Judas Jenkins for a retraction of the claim. His lawyer's letter to Judas Jenkins can be summed up by this one excerpt:

"[Y]ou correct false statements you made that Mr. Kaepernick was invited to the last players meeting."

157 Soon after, Judas Jenkins posted a message in the Players Coalition's group chat regarding Knee-sus lawyering up. It read:

"Heads up guys. I removed Kap from this chat. His attorneys have been contacting me and it seems clear to me that he is not interested in working under the Coalition. I think it's important that we keep him involved in what we do and he will still be invited to meetings that we have. But in regards to our decision making and communications between members of the Coalition, I think it's important to keep these things in house in the spirit of solidarity."

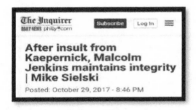

The Inquirer
DAILY NEWS philly*com — Subscribe — Log In — ☰

After insult from Kaepernick, Malcolm Jenkins maintains integrity | Mike Sielski
Posted: October 29, 2017 - 8:46 PM

158 The gloves were off as far as Knee-sus was concerned. Knee-sus had also accused Judas Jenkins of stealing his ideas, even though several members of the Players Coalition contended that Knee-sus never submitted any ideas to them.

159 Some people have assumed that Knee-sus insulted Judas Jenkins; he didn't! Knee-sus was merely speaking in tongues. And the words were a reminder to Judas Jenkins that he (Knee-sus) is the alpha and omega.

160 And when Rowdy Reid got the opportunity to confront Judas Jenkins on the football field after the Players Coalition's partnership deal, it got physical. Their teammates had to intervene.

161 After the game, Rowdy Reid called Judas Jenkins a *"sellout"* and *"neo-colonialist."* He maintained that Jenkins had sold out Knee-sus for thirty pieces of silver and *"capitalized on the situation."* Reid also called Jenkins a coward for hijacking *"the movement that was started by Colin to get his organization funded."*

162 In response to the dust-up between his former and present disciples, Knee-sus tweeted support for his darling devotee: *"Eric Reid!!! Enough said!!!"* He followed up the six exclamation points of love with the hashtag *"#ImwithReid."*

163 If only an NFL team had stood with Knee-sus the way he stood with Reid. Maybe then, he wouldn't have become a vagabond and NFL castaway.

164 His soft exile even led a columnist to write that Knee-sus *"has as much chance of playing quarterback again in the NFL as a police officer would of being convicted of killing a black man."*

165 He was crucified and made to bear his cross. And after slowly coming to grips with his fate, Knee-sus took solace in the belief that he was on the right side of ~~his story~~ history.

166 Be that as it may, Sports Illustrated magazine wanted to capture this exact moment in history when professional athletes, coaches, team leaders, etc. were highlighting social justice issues. The magazine utilized its popular cover to feature several prominent "woke" athletes such as Lebron James, who once referred to the NFL's Pharisees as *"old white men"* with a *"slave mentality."* [cxxxiii]

167 However, remarkably missing from the cover was the "wokest" player of them all; the player who was on Time magazine's cover in 2016 for igniting the movement. Knee-sus, the original Bender of the Knee and universal symbol of activist-athletes, was knowingly left off the cover.

168 This was a vile act of agnosticism! Even God Goodell was on the cover with his arms locked with basketball superstar Stephen Curry. Curry later candidly called the cover *"terrible,"* and decried:

"[I]f you don't have Kaepernick front and center on that, something's wrong." cxxxiv

169 When Sports Illustrated's Executive Editor clarified that the cover intended to showcase new voices because everyone already knew the originator (Knee-sus), the RGI's media arm accused him of "White-splaining." cxxxv

170 During his clarification for Knee-sus' absence, he stated:

"This debate, this issue, this protest movement, has sort of evolved even beyond Colin Kaepernick, and I think we saw a lot of people join the movement, for lack of a better term." [cxxxvi]

171 The editor's ~~sensible~~ sacrilegious statement sounded as if it was straight from the Gospel of Judas Jenkins. Despite Knee-sus not being on the cover, his presence still loomed over it — just like his presence loomed over the NFL's 2017 season even though he wasn't in it.

172 There was no consolation for being left off a sports cover for the movement he started, or left out of a league that he once starred in.

173 His career appeared to be without form, and void; and darkness was on the face of it. Yet, a glimmer of light hovered over it.

174 When the Carolina Panthers announced that the team would be for sale after the 2017 season, Diddy, a music mogul, tweeted his intent to buy the team. And if that happened, he promised to throw Knee-sus a lifeline:

"I will immediately address the Colin Kaepernick situation and put him in the running for next year's starting quarterback."

175 Knee-sus, sensing that this was a chance to turn career tragedy into triumph, responded to Diddy's intentions on Twitter with: *"I want in on the ownership group! Let's make it happen!"*

176 Their entrepreneurial and ambitious talk of a collaboration to buy the Panthers as the first minority-majority owners of an NFL franchise did what it was intended to do: keep Knee-sus relevant. But in the end, it did nothing to change his career's trajectory.

177 When the 2017 regular season officially concluded, *"56 different quarterbacks"* had started NFL games.[cxxxvii] Many of whom had losing records or never played in an NFL game. On the flipside, Knee-sus went unsigned and deemed unqualified to even carry a clipboard on the sideline.

178 His career was dead, and a coroner wasn't needed to make the declaration. It was now time to focus on the afterlife.

CHAPTER IV

Resurrection in the Afterlife

¹ O ye, of little faith. Did you not think that Knee-sus would triumph over his tribulations?

² You must learn to feed your faith and starve your fears as Knee-sus did. He never lost faith that he'd find others to blame for his murky situation.

³ Sure, his football career as an NFL signal-caller came to an abrupt end in 2017. However, through faith, his vocation as a virtue signal-caller didn't end, it strengthened and even expanded.

⁴ For instance, Knee-sus spent Thanksgiving 2017 on Alcatraz Island[cxxxviii] celebrating the annual Indigenous People Sunrise Ceremony also known as *"Unthanksgiving Day."* It's a tradition that commemorates the American Indians who participated in the occupation of Alcatraz between 1969-71. American Indian leaders presently want the island and former

prison to be repurposed as an Indian cultural center and school.

⁵ On that "Unthanksgiving Day," Knee-sus gave a feather-fitted resistance sermon. He preached:

"I realize that our fight is the same fight. We're all fighting for our justice, for our freedom, and realizing that we're in this fight together makes it all the more powerful. If there's one thing that I take away from today and seeing the beauty of everybody out here, it's that we're only getting stronger every day, we're only getting larger and larger every day. I see the strength in everybody. The dancing, the rituals – that is our resistance. We continue to fight. We continue to fight for justice. We fight for our freedom, and we continue on that path." cxxxix

⁶ Through his victim-centric sermon, he connected with their struggle (though not the financial part of it). See, as a multi-millionaire, he has first-class reservations everywhere, unlike those participants who live on reservations.

⁷ The year 2017 also afforded him with free time to deliver "one size fits all" victim-centric sermons to whatever crowd would listen. It didn't matter if the crowd was

Indians, Cowboys, Jews, or Gentiles; as along as good publicity resulted and the message embraced.

8 God Goodell and the NFL's Pharisees laughably thought that by evicting Knee-sus from the NFL's pearly gates, he'd dwell in purgatory. Au contraire! Knee-sus dwelled in a state of jubilation because his cup had runneth over with opportunities. The only limbo he experienced was doing the limbo dance while getting into limos.

9 The book that he had been shopping (not the Gospel of Knee-sus) was picked up for one-million-dollars and slated to be released in 2019 along with a speaking tour.[cxl]

10 And remember when Sports Illustrated ghosted him on its cover? Soon after, GQ magazine featured and honored him (alone) on its cover as the *"2017 Citizen of the Year."*

11 The honor ~~should've~~ could've easily gone to J.J. Watt, a future NFL Hall of Famer who raised more than thirty-seven million dollars for Hurricane Harvey victims in Houston.[cxli] Instead, GQ went with the hot ~~hand~~ knee to exalt, even though the only thing Knee-sus raised was ~~division~~ awareness.

12 On its cover, GQ made sure that Knee-sus looked GQ with a "woke" vibe. He was dressed in black like ~~Ms. Mary Mack~~ the Black Panthers of old with his signature Afro. I'm not critical, but his afro was missing one vital accessory: a metal hair pick with a black fist sticking from it. He also had the stylings of Shaft, who was a fictional character from the 1970's blaxploitation film. Unlike Shaft, Knee-sus ~~is~~ isn't playing a character.

[13] The GQ article accurately acknowledged that he *"will not be silenced."* Yes! Vengeance was his, and he would repay!

[14] Sports Illustrated later became believers and repented for its previous transgression against Knee-sus. And as a token of goodwill, the magazine honored him with its Muhammad Ali Legacy award.[cxlii] Beyoncé, the "woke" superstar singer and ardent supporter of his mission, was picked to be the presenter.

[15] Knee-sus showed mercy to the magazine and accepted its peace offering. He then utilized the moment to remind Sports Illustrated and other cynics that:

"[W]ith or without the NFL's platform, I will continue to work for the people because my platform is the people."

16 And when the world's top sports apparel company needed a marketable athlete for its newest ad campaign, it didn't tap its Rolodex of recognizable, non-controversial athletes. Nike went off-script and pursued the lone athlete who was primarily recognizable because of his controversial knee and polarizing unemployment status.

17 Despite his football career being crucified by age thirty, Nike calculatedly chose Knee-sus to be the face of its thirtieth-anniversary "Just Do It" ad campaign.

18 This was Nike's second major decision regarding Knee-sus. He had been on its product endorsement team since his 2011 rookie season,[cxliii] but the company seriously contemplated severing ties with him after the Year of the Knee. Nike ultimately decided that it would be best to keep him on the roster to avoid any potential backlash for releasing him.

19 Knee-sus' ad made its television debut during the NFL's 2018 season opener. The timing was perfect. His revolution was being televised while he existed in the hereafter. It was a ~~strange~~ glorious sight to behold.

20 The ad was sweet revenge against God Goodell, the NFL's Pharisees, and detractors. It was also emotionally and financially lucrative.

21 On that day of reckoning, Knee-sus had hand-delivered a heavy heaping of karma to the unholy trinity of God Goodell, the NFL's Pharisees, and detractors. He temporarily broke their spirit while permanently repairing his public relations image.

22 Jim Brown, a Hall of Fame running back, and face on the Mount Rushmore of black activist-athletes, once said that Knee-sus needed to choose between activism and athletics.[cxliv]

23 Well, with all due respect to Mr. Brown, Knee-sus' choice was clear, especially since his movement procured mainstream corporate sponsorship. Recall, in the Year of the Knee, Knee-sus decisively traded his helmet for a halo. Now, his halo had Nike's Swoosh logo on it.

24 Sports-writing ~~heroes~~ heretics, such as Jason Whitlock (who once dubbed Knee-sus as *"Martin Luther Cornrow"*), took issue with Knee-sus because he didn't bend the knee for the National Anthem, yet shamelessly got on all fours for Nike. Whitlock tweeted:

"Told y'all from Day One this has always been about the money. All of it.

Revolutionaries aren't sponsored by major corporations. It's been a hustle from the giddy-up." [cxlv]

25 Knee-sus' new Nike contract was described as a "top of the line" deal for football players (let alone, a former football player) and potentially worth millions of dollars a year. [cxlvi]

26 With such a sizable amount of money invested in Knee-sus, Nike now needed to ensure an equally sizable return on its investment. Capitalizing off of his movement was Nike's next maneuver after openly attaching itself to appear "woke."

27 Although the ad itself targeted Knee-sus' followers and those who devotedly stand in long lines for Air Jordans, Nike's marketing department created the ad's slogan to serve a dual purpose. The slogan intended to appeal to his supporters while angering non-supporters.

28 This strategy ensured dissension. And from the dissension, invaluable publicity would be generated without Nike spending a cent — as the publicity generated dollars and cents.

29 As sure as Hell is hot, this Fortune 500 multinational corporation is a master of playing both sides of a fence for capitalistic gain.

30 For instance, while Nike was financially backing Knee-sus, it extended its NFL uniform and apparel deal with God Goodell to the year 2028.[cxlvii]

31 Nike also donates money to both the Democratic and Republican Parties. It doesn't put all its eggs in one basket. Or as PETA (People for the Ethical Treatment of Animals) recommends the idiom be reworded as, *"berries in a bowl."*[cxlviii] Regardless of the expression, in 2018, Nike contributed three times as many eggs/berries to the basket/bowl of Republican candidates than Democratic candidates.[cxlix] I digress.

32 *"Believe in something, even if it means sacrificing everything"* is the nine-word slogan that Nike devised. The phrase is simplistic deepness. Its simplicity makes the slogan easy to remember, and the deepness evokes emotions to make supporters reach deep into their pockets.

33 And if you open your mind's eye, you'll see that the slogan is basically a fusion of the mottos *"What Would Jesus Do"* and *"Just Do It."*

34 Without a doubt, ~~Pat Tillman~~ Knee-sus unequivocally embodies this nine-word slogan.

35 Admittedly, Knee-sus' embrace of Nike's *"Believe in something, even if it means sacrificing everything"* slogan appears to be a departure from his initial mission statement to fight racial oppression and police brutality against black people.

36 But listen to reason! Granted, Knee-sus' Nike ad has nothing to do with fighting police brutality or racial oppression. Even so, his original overview remains tethered to his ministry. He hasn't changed! He's $imply evolving with the time$ by exhibiting PAY-triotism! Besides, what does it profit a man to gain the whole world, yet forfeit his ~~Nike soles~~ soul?

37 Nike's gamble to put Knee-sus' ad in motion to cause commotion turned out to be a winner. The uproar made landfall like a Category Five hurricane. Listed are some instances of the outcry.

- People again burned their Nike apparel.[cl]
- An Alabama pastor cut up his Nike gear during a sermon.[cli]
- A Missouri College discarded its Nike athletic uniforms as an act of *"country over company."* [clii]

- A boycott was called by police organizations, including the National Association of Police Organizations (an interest group that represents more than 241,000 officers).[cliii]
- A mayor of a Louisiana town tried to ban Nike products from being purchased for the city's recreational facilities.[cliv]
- President Orange Herod venomously tweeted: *"Just like the NFL, whose ratings have gone WAY DOWN, Nike is getting absolutely killed with anger and boycotts. I wonder if they had any idea that it would be this way? As far as the NFL is concerned, I just find it hard to watch, and always will, until they stand for the FLAG!"*

38 The outcome from the outrage yielded massive income. Nike's online sales surged and its shares reached at an all-time high after rebounding from a slight dip. The ad campaign generated record engagement with the brand,[clv] and one Wall Street analyst described it as *"a stroke of genius."* CBS deemed Knee-sus to be Nike's "*$6 billion man.*"

39 The public's favorite piece of Knee-sus' Nike garment was the long sleeve, black shirt with his name across the back in reflective, metallic lettering, and signature wooly-haired afro on the front. It sold out within hours of release.[clvi]

40 Take heed! Only Nike shalt make unto thee any graven image of Knee-sus! Anyone else will payeth dearly because Knee-sus has a pending trademark for his image.[clvii] The Chosen One must safeguard against any unauthorized usage, which is why I'm explaining rather than showing his signature image. I don't want to incur his ~~wrath~~ legal wrath.

41 After suffering so many losses in his football career and then losing the career itself, Knee-sus strived to be undefeated in the afterlife. His intestinal fortitude eventually led to a winning streak in the afterlife not experienced since reaching the 2012 Super Bowl and subsequent 2013 championship game.

42 His greatest afterlife win was the preliminary legal victory over God Goodell and the NFL's Pharisees.[clviii] To their dismay, an arbitrator ruled that Knee-sus' grievance case could proceed against them. The two parties eventually reached a settlement before the case went to trial. The details of the agreement were confidential,[clix] but NFL officials speculated that Knee-sus could receive as much as $80 million for his suffering. In translation, his bread is poised to multiply exponentially, and it likely won't be shared with the multitudes. However, some of that ~~multi-grain~~ multi-million-dollar bread will indubitably be broken with his most trusted disciple, Rowdy Reid, who was also included in the $ettlement.

43 Recognize that this colossal estimate of ~~hush~~ settlement money from God Goodell and the NFL's Pharisees wasn't a tithe to Knee-sus; it was reparations and a donation to prevent more bad omens from happening to them. Although God Goodell and the NFL's Pharisees had won the initial battle to oust Knee-sus, he won the war! He also maintained reverence from the media, disciples, and followers. They didn't dare question him for ending the conflict in the same "sell-out" manner that Rowdy Reid had earlier castigated the Players Coalition for doing.

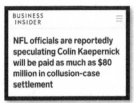

CNBC

Colin Kaepernick reaches settlement in national anthem kneeling collusion case against NFL

Dan Mangan | @_DanMangan
Published 2:06 PM ET Fri, 15 Feb 2019

BUSINESS INSIDER

NFL officials are reportedly speculating Colin Kaepernick will be paid as much as $80 million in collusion-case settlement

⁴⁴ And the good omens continued to manifest for Knee-sus. He had encountered a phenomenon that often occurs posthumously with dead celebrities. His net worth and followers were increasing extraordinarily fast as if he had physically died when only his football career kicked the bucket.

⁴⁵ Not only did his finances and clout grow, but the discipleship grew to include a diverse group of influential people who weren't athletes. One common and fitting attribute amongst many of these tastemakers was their birthplaces being cities where black deaths from black thugs historically dwarfed the demises of Knee-groes.

⁴⁶ This mixed-bag of disciples also included influencers who plainly recognized the branding benefits of being associated with Knee-sus.

⁴⁷ Rihanna, an international songstress from Barbados, declined an offer from God Goodell to headline the NFL's Super Bowl LIII halftime show.[clx] Although the Super Bowl is one of the most coveted platforms for musicians because of its unmatched exposure, she turned it down to stand with Knee-sus under his (sing it with me) *"umbrella, ella, ella, eh, eh, eh."*

48 Chart-topping female rapper, Cardi B, also refused to perform at the Super Bowl until the NFL *"hires Colin Kaepernick back."* She took her vow to Knee-sus on stage at the MTV Video Music Awards, saying:

"Colin Kaepernick, as long as you kneel with us, we're gonna be standing for you, baby. That's right, I said it." [clxi]

49 Following the lead of these musical nuns for Knee-sus was Peabody award-winning comedian, Amy Schumer. She pledged allegiance to Knee-sus on Instagram by informing her seven-million followers of the planned non-appearance in any Super Bowl LIII ads. And the comedienne wasn't joking when writing:

"I wonder why more white players aren't kneeling. Once you witness the truly deep inequality and endless racism people of color face in our country, not to mention the police brutality and murders. Why not kneel next to your brothers? Otherwise how are you not complicit?" [clxii]

50 If an Apostles' Creed for Knee-sus existed, I wonder if it would've worked on Apollo Creed, the American-flag wearing boxer from the Rocky film series. I doubt it. Clubber Lang (Mr. T's character) is debatable though. Since there isn't an Apostles' Creed for recitation, the apostles alternatively recite or hashtag Knee-sus' name. This form of fealty peaked during the lead-up to Super Bowl LIII. The apostles had aggressively tried to dissuade entertainers (especially black entertainers) from performing. They'd rather them perform at toilet bowls. The apostles were tenacious, and with a Jehovah Witness-like zeal, repeatedly knocked on the doors of potential performers. When they knocked on Travis Scott's door to sell the kingdom of Knee-sus, the famous rapper pretended not to be inside (a common tactic) and didn't answer. However, he did answer the call from God Goodell to perform at the Super Bowl. Because he chose God Goodell's secular calling over Knee-sus' ~~crying~~ calling, his name was removed from Knee-sus' Book of Life. Scott's short-term, unrighteous decision likely faces long-term reprisals from the apostles' invisible yet influential hand in the music business.

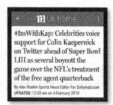
51 Beto O'Rourke, an up-and-coming Texas Democratic politician who some have called the "new Barack Obama,"[clxiii] was also eager to cape for Knee-sus. When Beto was asked about players kneeling during the National Anthem, he responded:

"I can think of nothing more American than to peacefully stand up, or take a knee, for your rights, anytime, anywhere, or any place." [clxiv]

52 His comment went viral, which prompted several of Knee-sus' high-profile acolytes to rush to social media and welcome him to the faith.

53 NBA superstar, Lebron James, tweeted (to his nearly forty-two million Twitter followers), *"Salute Beto O' Rourke for the candid thoughtful words!"* [clxv]

54 Serial Emmy award-winning talk show host, Ellen DeGeneres, tweeted to Beto O' Rourke (from her Twitter account with seventy-six million followers) *"I would like to meet you."* [clxvi]

55 Realize, this is why Knee-sus never held a last supper (or first) with his apostles before or after his cruci-fiction. The disciples are innumerable! Even IKEA or Legos wouldn't be able to assemble a table large enough to accommodate them all.

56 On November 2, 2018, a female disciple was able to blindside Knee-sus' former team in his honor. She hid in plain sight as a cheerleader and did something during the National Anthem that Knee-sus would've done had he not been crucified.

57 The dedicated soul took a knee.

58 The local news reported that it was the second time a member of the cheerleading squad (known as Gold Rush) had taken a knee.[clxvii] The other time happened before a Christmas Eve game in 2017.

59 Interestingly, this cheerleader's kneeling occurred a couple of weeks after the 49ers released an online photo gallery that commemorated the franchise's nearly seventy-year history of battles against the division rival Green Bay Packers.[clxviii]

60 The nostalgic gallery included snapshots of every prominent 49ers' player who partook in those epic battles. Ahem, almost every prominent 49ers' player was featured. Knee-sus was suspiciously absent from the photo gallery.

61 The team had once again, relegated him to the bench.

62 What fools these mortals be! In his first playoff start against the Green Bay Packers, Knee-sus, who was then known as the Word, threw two touchdowns and ran for another two. He also set an NFL single-game rushing yards record for a quarterback. clxix

63 Knee-sus' legendary performance was one for the NFL's record books, but somehow, not the team's photo book. ¯_(ツ)_/¯

64 When his followers learned of the blatant omission, they immediately took the team to the social media woodshed. Knee-sus Nation wanted a blood sacrifice for this sinful act but was willing to settle for the photo gallery being cast into the Lake of Fire.

65 As a result, the team endeavored to explain the inexplicable. They wrote:

"Unfortunately there were a handful of obvious misses in this gallery posted by our website team and we appreciate them being brought to our attention. The 49ers organization has tremendous respect and gratitude for the contributions Colin made to our team over the years. We have fond

memories of those games and that should have been displayed on our website. This oversight does not properly reflect the appreciation our ownership and this team have for Colin. " clxx

66 Two photos of Knee-sus were hurriedly added to the gallery. However, it was too late; the photos were no consolation for the overt disrespect of Knee-sus in the afterlife.

67 Of course, Knee-sus really didn't need the recognition from his former football team. He just wanted what the franchise owed him: respect. He was content with the overwhelming love and recognition received in the hereafter from non-football organizations.

68 Listen, not only was he the Racial Grievance Industry's MVP (Most Valuable ~~Pawn~~ Person) but Amnesty International, the global human rights organization, gave him its highest honor: the Ambassador of Conscience award.clxxi Years ago, this distinguished award was also given to Nelson Mandela, the former President of South Africa.

69 The Ambassador of Conscience honor came on top of his Courageous Advocate award from the American Civil Liberties Union (ACLU). And after receiving a standing ovation for the award, Knee-sus told the adoring crowd of limousine-Leftists what they came to hear.

"We must confront systemic oppression as a doctor would a disease. You identify it, you call it out, you treat it, and you defeat it. We all have an obligation no matter the risk, and regardless of reward, to stand up for our fellow men and women who are being oppressed, with an understanding that human rights cannot be compromised." clxxii

70 Amazingly, Leftists never tire of sanctimonious talks. The venerable economist, Thomas Sowell, best described this behavior: *"People are never more sincere than when they assume their own moral superiority."* clxxiii

71 When Knee-sus received an honorary W.E.B. Du Bois Medal from Harvard University for his influence on black culture and history, he delivered a parable (of sorts) that explained Nike's ad slogan. It was a perspective that only his staunchest supporters would comprehend. He preached:

"And I go to what recently happened with the Nike campaign, where 'Believe in something, even if it means sacrificing everything' quote became huge. As I reflected on that, it made me

think, if we all believe in something, we won't have to sacrifice everything." clxxiv

72 ~~Wait... What~~? Amen! Although he can't turn water into wine, his whining flowed like water on that day.

73 Without question, Knee-sus was living his best life in the afterlife. The awards, international recognition, unearthly income, flourishing followers, and the other derivatives of his arduous journey, had transitioned with him.

74 Still, it was the lack of a destination that secretly haunted Knee-sus. I don't mean his ministry's lack of a destination (that's already predetermined); I'm talking about the unknown career destination had he not taken a knee. His supporters also wonder about that alternate reality.

75 The fixed fact of the matter is that Knee-sus is where he's supposed to be! Nevertheless, he can find solace in knowing that his name will continue to be invoked whenever an NFL team finds itself in desperate need of a quarterback.

76 This was the situation as recently as November and December of 2018. The first and second-string quarterbacks for the Washington Redskins suffered season-ending injuries. And because the team was still in

playoff contention, finding a solid, veteran quarterback became imperative.

77 Knee-sus was the most prominent person floated as a candidate,[clxxv] but legitimate concerns lingered. Did he have the desire to leave the afterlife to play? Was he in football shape? Would he stop his sideline pastime in a town where President Orange Herod resides, and for a team whose owner is anti-kneeling? Would he violate his treaty with the *"Unthanksgiving Day"* peoples to play for a team whose name they believe denigrates Native Americans?

78 The sobering answers to those questions were apparently yes, yes, yes, yes, and yes. In fact, several media sources reported that Knee-sus was willing to play for "any NFL team" if offered, including the Washington Redskins.

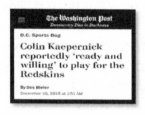
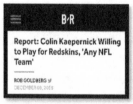

79 The Redskins had internal discussions about Knee-sus but never reached out to him. They decided to go in a different direction by signing retired, Heisman-winning quarterback, Doug Flutie.[clxxvi]

[80] Nah, just kidding, Flutie wasn't signed, but the Redskins did deny Knee-sus. And for what it's worth, Flutie wouldn't have been any worse than the quarterback who was signed. The newly-signed quarterback was an out-of-work journeyman who had played for twelve teams (some of them twice) within his ten-year career — and hadn't thrown a pass in an NFL game since 2011. The journeyman was so unfamiliar with the team that he resorted to using the *"Madden"* video game to learn his new teammates' names.

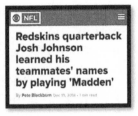

[81] For Knee-sus, it was Déjà vu. He had again lost a job to a journeyman. In my humble opinion, if Knee-sus really wants to scratch that itch and play football again, he should consider the Canadian Football League (CFL). Flutie and other NFL quarterbacks found success by playing on its wider field. Joining the CFL could possibly result in a Lazarus-like resurrection for his career! Another benefit is the lack of the U.S. National Anthem! He'd be able to utilize the sideline for its intended purpose and not

have to agonize through the Star-Spangled Banner. On paper, the CFL is nirvana.

82 Another alternative is a new professional football league called the Alliance of American Football (AAF).[clxxvii] It was founded in 2018 with 2019 being its inaugural season. There are eight teams, and they play a twelve-week season that begins after the NFL's Super Bowl ends. It's headquartered in San Francisco, which may be a sign for Knee-sus to return to his former ~~kneeling~~ stomping ground, though he might want to check the anthem policy in advance. AAF reportedly did reach out to him and another popular kneeler, Tim Tebow, who knelt for a different reason.

83 Knee-sus purportedly responded to AAF's request with a demand for $20 million to suit up.[clxxviii] Contrast his salary demand to the three-year, $250,000 non-guaranteed deals that all AAF players receive,[clxxix] and clearly, Knee-sus was telling AAF to take a long walk on a short plank.

84 There was a time when returning to the NFL was the only miracle that Knee-sus wanted to perform. Nowadays, he claims to be enjoying eternal life without football and content with his spirit haunting the NFL, the sports world, and businesses that bet against him.

85 Just know that if Knee-sus ever returns to the gridiron, it would be like a thief in the night.

CHAPTER V

Church of the Eternal Victim

¹ Don't be disheartened that Chapter V is the closing chapter of Knee-sus' gospel. It's actually the opening of the victim-centric path! Behold! There's a specific reason why this sanctified scroll has only five chapters. In Roman Numerals, the number five is represented as the letter V, and in the Church of the Eternal Victim (COTEV), the letter V is the most powerful letter of the most powerful word: victim.

² V is also for Vendetta and the symbol for Vanadium — a hard, malleable transition metal with an atomic number of 23. Observe that $2+3=5$, which again, is the letter V's Roman Numeral value. This is supreme mathematics! Vibranium is another forceful metal and only found in the black utopian country of Wakanda, which white people think is fictional. Vibranium possesses an unnatural ability to leverage and control kinetic energy.

[3] Understand that adherents in COTEV (which is largely comprised of American blacks who believe that racism is their utmost problem) need to be ~~hard-headed~~ hard and ~~gullible~~ malleable like Vanadium. Furthermore, they must maintain an unnatural ability to leverage and control victimhood with Vibranium-like precision. On this path where disgruntlement has precedence over empowerment, members should wear victimhood on their outfits like the Black Panther wore Vibranium on his.

[4] People often ask about COTEV's beginnings and are surprised to learn that it is not new or a brick and mortar institution. COTEV has been in existence for at least a century.

[5] In fact, a ~~free-thinker~~ diabolical critic of the church named Booker T Washington led a smear campaign in the 20th century against the COTEV prophets of old. In his 1911 book, "My Larger Education, Being Chapters from My Experience," he warned:

"There is another class of colored people who make a business of keeping the troubles, the wrongs, and the hardships of the Negro race before the public. ... Some of these people do not want the Negro to lose his grievances, because they do not want to lose their jobs ... There is a certain class of race-

problem solvers who don't want the patient to get well." clxxx

5 In that same chapter, which is ~~not~~ coincidentally Chapter V, Washington extended his criticism of the *"race-problem solvers"* a few paragraphs later:

"I am afraid that there is a certain class of race-problem solvers who don't want the patient to get well, because as long as the disease holds out they have not only an easy means of making a living, but also an easy medium through which to make themselves prominent before the public."

6 Fortunately for Booker T. Washington, he wasn't burned at the stake for his heresy. To this day, Washington's legacy continues to be a thorn in COTEV's side because COTEV's mission of placing racial aggrievement over racial achievement hasn't changed.

9 But because black advancement in the United States is undeniably obvious, COTEV had to slowly transition from the dated talking points found in its Old Testament of Racial Grievances and incorporate the contemporary talking points from the New Testament as brought forth by Knee-sus.

10 COTEV's acceptance of Knee-sus as its lord and ~~savior~~ savant even has the blessings of senior pastors such as Reverend Jesse Jackson.

[11] Reverend Jackson, who had leaned heavily on the Old Testament of Racial Grievances for his entire career, mixed talking points from both the Old and New Testaments of Racial Grievances (and created a ~~Bible~~ Cry-ble of sorts) to defend Knee-sus. He equated cotton-picking slaves to million-dollar NFL and NBA (National Basketball Association) players:

"To go from picking cotton balls to picking footballs and basketballs without freedom is not very much progress — it's just a lateral move." [clxxxi]

[12] Knee-sus, himself, had struggled with lateral moves and passes during the final years of his abbreviated football career; but seamlessly moved from the football game to the blame game. And like Jesus, the humble carpenter declared two thousand years ago, *"On this rock, I will build my church,"* [clxxxii]

Knee-sus, the quiet quarterback (whose passes hammered the turf in carpenter-like fashion) declared football as his rock to further build the Church of the Eternal Victim.

[13] As a result, Jesus the Christ brought Christianity, and Knee-sus the Victim (sometimes called Knee-sus the Niner) delivered Victimanity. Both visionaries are the central figures of their respective religions.

[14] At the core of Victimanity are seven commandments. Ten commandments are too many. These short seven commandments are wisely enumerated dogmatic COTEV principles symbolized by Knee-sus' jersey number.

1. Nothing is ever thy fault. Thy is always a victim of circumstance.
2. Every down is a punting down. Punt away responsibility.
3. The most valuable real estate is in the hood — victimhood.
4. Never partake of the Forbidden Fruit called accountability. Lest not even touch it, or ye shall suffer.
5. A problem shared is a problem halved, so give thy problematic half away and make it a whole problem for someone else.

6. Judgment day is every day. Therefore, be sure to judge others for your short-comings.
7. Thy is not thy own worst enemy; the enemy is always external.

[15] In addition to these commandments, COTEV members rely on a handy reference guide known as the Five-Finger formula. In the Five- Finger formula, each finger is assigned a victim-based tenet that further instills Victimanity.

- The pinky signifies a pinky promise that one's best ability isn't answerability.
- The ring finger indicates a commitment to victimhood.
- The middle finger is for non-Knee-groes.
- The index or pointer finger is for pointing at everyone except oneself.
- The thumb is for hitchhiking between grievances, especially racial grievances.

[16] Remember, the helping hand is not at the end of one's arm but someone else's. It's incumbent upon followers to stay knee-deep in victimhood, and if needed, tear the knee's Anterior Cruciate Ligament (ACL) for this objective to be accomplished. Victimanity should be practiced valiantly.

17 And to the victims who don't realize that they're victims, the hour is at hand. Come and sup with COTEV and get baptized in the reliable river of victimhood. At COTEV, salvation is only a knee-bend away, and there's no need to repent for anything because nothing is ever your fault. COTEV is the no-fault church!

18 Just as a poor workman always blames his tools, you are the black stone that was rejected by builders. But at COTEV you'll be family. And by joining the growing flock, you get to wallow in misery with our choir a.k.a. Sympathy Symphony and sing the same sad songs about *"overcoming."* Cheese isn't served with our whine, but those heartstrings will be serviceably tugged.

19 If singing isn't desirable, simply come and help to spread COTEV's universal values:

- The *"us versus them"* attitude
- Racial harmony through racial discord
- Truth-telling by way of lying
- Standing by taking a knee — the most obvious value as revealed by the church's avatar of aggrievement.

20 Even though America is knee-deep in pressing problems such as the ballooning national debt, just ignore that dire reality and ease on down the road of victimhood. Bend the knee for COTEV's race-based reality and help race relations erode, police be demonized, and America be despised.

²¹ Behold! This is the final verse just as the twenty-first verse is the last verse of the Revelation of Jesus Christ. Twenty-one is also Knee-sus' jersey number (seven) times three (7x3=21). The three represents the three phases of his ministry: Revelation, Cruci-fiction, and Resurrection. All proper praises and salutations are due to that ~~selfish~~ selfless entity, the high priest of havoc, who cashed-out in Victimanity's name. May his ~~greed~~ grace be with you, and the main take away from this gospel be a knee. Amen.

Your humble, truth-teller,

Taleeb Starkes

Taleeb@TheUncivilWar.info

i "Colin Kaepernick laments 49ers' Super Bowl loss, vows to improve" - washingtontimes.com, 2/5/13
ii "San Francisco 49ers QB Colin Kaepernick Wins "Greatness on the Road" Award Presented by Courtyard at "2nd Annual NFL Honors" - travelprnews.com, 2/4/13
iii "Kaepernick Wins Breakthrough Athlete Trophy At ESPY Awards" - sanfrancisco.cbslocal.com, 7/18/13
iv "Jaworski: Kaepernick could be one of the greatest ever" - nfl.com, 8/22/13
v "CK1: Colin Kaepernick" - gq.com, 8/14/13
vi "Colin Kaepernick signs six-year, $126 million extension with 49ers" - cbssports.com, 6/4/14
vii "8 things you should know about sports scholarships" - cbsnews.com, 9/20/12
viii "Colin Kaepernick Biography" - biography.com
ix "Race Matters: Biracial 49er's QB Colin Kaepernick Fined $11,000 For Using N-Word On The Field During Game" - bossip.com, 9/22/14
x "Colin Kaepernick uses image of Texas floods to trash-talk Texans fans" - sbnation.com, 5/26/15
xi "7 facts that explain why Colin Kaepernick was just benched for Blaine Gabbert" - ftw.usatoday.com, 11/3/15
xii "7 facts that explain why Colin Kaepernick was just benched for Blaine Gabbert" - ftw.usatoday.com, 11/3/15
xiii "You probably forgot how bad Colin Kaepernick was last year" - foxsports.com, 11/15/16
xiv "Jerry Rice: Benching Kaepernick 'could energize' 49ers" - nbcsports.com, 10/28/15
xv "Young's advice: Tie up Kaepernick's legs" - espn.com, 6/4/14
xvi "Niners bench Colin Kaepernick; Blaine Gabbert to start" - nfl.com, 11/2/15
xvii "The End is Near for Flawed QBs Griffin and Kaepernick" – si.com, 3/3/16
xviii "Report: Colin Kaepernick asks 49ers for permission to seek a trade" - cbssports.com, 2/25/16
xix "Blaine Gabbert, Colin Kaepernick splitting snaps to start training camp" - ninersnation.com, 7/31/16
xx "Chip Kelly-Colin Kaepernick marriage terrifies defensive coaches" - nfl.com, 1/22/16
xxi "Tomsula: Kaepernick benching will allow him to 'step back and breathe'" - cbssports.com, 11/4/15
xxii "Kaepernick talks benching: 'Don't believe that's accurate'" - nbcsports.com, 11/6/15
xxiii "All Eyez on Me" - wikipedia.org
xxiv "Colin Kaepernick explains why he sat during national anthem" - nfl.com, 8/27/16
xxv "Red ink: The high human cost of the Cuban revolution" - Red ink: The high human cost of the Cuban revolution, 12/1/16
xxvi "Unrepentant hypocrite Colin Kaepernick defends Fidel Castro" – miamiherald.com, 11/25/16
xxvii "List Of Countries By Literacy Rate" - worldatlas.com, 9/14/18
xxviii "Unrepentant hypocrite Colin Kaepernick defends Fidel Castro" – miamiherald.com, 11/25/16
xxix "LOOK: Colin Kaepernick's practice socks appear to disrespect the police" - cbssports.com, 8/31/16
xxx ""Pigs in a blanket" chant at Minnesota fair riles police" - cbsnews.com, 8/31/15
xxxi "49ers' Colin Kaepernick transcript: 'I'll continue to sit'" - sfchronicle.com, 8/28/16
xxxii "COLIN KAEPERNICK PROTEST SO BIG, IT DESERVED COVER... Says Time Mag" - tmz.com, 9/22/16
xxxiii "Irreconcilable differences: Why the Players Coalition split apart" - theundefeated.com, 2/2/18
xxxiv "Athletes who have joined Colin Kaepernick's national anthem protest" - foxsports.com, 10/20/16
xxxv "USWNT star Megan Rapinoe takes knee in solidarity with Kaepernick" - cnn.com, 9/5/16
xxxvi "High school players taking knee for national anthem across country" - usatodayhss.com, 9/10/16
xxxvii "As Kaepernick's protest spreads, SF prep team takes a knee" - sfchronicle.com, 9/15/16
xxxviii "High school football team lies down with hands up as Colin Kaepernick kneels during national anthem" - sbnation.com, 9/24/16
xxxix "Michigan, Michigan State players raise fists during national anthem" - espn.com, 9/25/16
xl "ECU chancellor, Gov. McCrory speak out about band members kneeling" - witn.com, 10/3/16
xli "West Virginia Tech volleyball players kneel during national anthem" - wchstv.com, 9/7/16
xlii "Prior to game, Rose-Ivey told team of his decision to kneel for anthem" - journalstar.com, 9/24/16
xliii "QUARTERBACKS 2016" - footballoutsiders.com, 7/28/17
xliv "49ers Announce 2016 Team Award Recipients" - 49ers.com, 12/30/16
xlv "Colin Kaepernick sets NFL record for quarterback futility in loss to Bears" - washingtonpost.com, 12/4/16
xlvi "49ers Colin Kaepernick's surprise benching doesn't prevent 11th straight loss" - mercurynews.com, 12/4/16
xlvii "49ers, Colin Kaepernick restructure deal into one-year contract with player option" - cbssports.com, 10/12/16
xlviii "Colin Kaepernick's biggest problem? Performance, not politics" - espn.com, 3/20/17
xlix "Matthew 15:24" – King James Bible
l "Amnesty International's Ambassador of Conscience Award Transcript of speech" - amnesty.nl, 4/21/18
li "Colin Kaepernick explains why he sat during national anthem" – nfl.com, 8/27/16
lii "Shooting of Terence Crutcher" – Wikipedia.org
liii Washington Post Data Base - 2016
liv "Colin Kaepernick shakes off death threats, seeks justice in Terence Crutcher killing" - mercurynews.com, 9/20/16
lv "Body found burned in alley ID'd as 15-year-old boy" - abc7chicago.com, 9/20/16
lvi "Colin Kaepernick explains why he sat during national anthem" – nfl.com, 8/27/16
lvii "Expanded Homicide Data Table 1" - ucr.fbi.gov, 2017
lviii "Mother of Baton Rouge's latest gun violence victim felt he was safer serving in Iraq" - theadvocate.com, 5/3/18
lix "'I'm not supposed to be burying my child:' Kent mother loses second child to shooting" - komonews.com, 2/2/18
lx "Father loses three children to violence" - wgrz.com, 6/14/17
lxi "Mark 6:4" - New American Standard Bible
lxii "Wisconsin GOP spikes Colin Kaepernick's name from Black History Month resolution" - nbcnews.com, 2/13/19
lxiii "Colin Kaepernick to be honored by Milwaukee after Republicans in Madison reject effort to recognize him" - jsonline.com, 2/15/19
lxiv "Can We Fight Milwaukee's Gun Violence Epidemic By Treating It Like A Public Health Crisis?" - milwaukeemag.com, 4/27/18
lxv "Bullets exacted terrible toll on children, African Americans" - wisconsinwatch.org, 1/11/15
lxvi "Spate of Milwaukee homicides have one thing in common – arguments that escalate into violence" - jsonline.com, 9/8/18
lxvii "Officials cite Milwaukee shooting victim's criminal record" - apnews.com, 8/15/16
lxviii "Milwaukee Unrest Continues Through 2nd Night, 1 Person Reported Shot" - web.archive.org, 8/15/16
lxix "Death of Sandra Bland" - wikipedia.org, 7/13/15
lxx "13-year-old who wrote essay on gun violence killed by stray bullet in her home" - washingtonpost.com, 11/22/18
lxxi "Washington Post Database" - washingtonpost.com, 2016-2018
lxxii "After hitting deadly peak in 2015, Milwaukee homicides decline for third year in a row" - jsonline.com, 12/31/18
lxxiii "Is Jacksonville still murder capital of Florida?" - news4jax.com, 6/20/18
lxxiv "Washington Post Report: Miami Among The Worst Cities For Solving Homicides" - wlrn.org, 6/6/18
lxxv "Mother of Jazmine Barnes says man 'intentionally' killed 7-year-old daughter while leaving Walmart in Texas" - abc7news.com, 12/31/18

lxxvi "Activist raises reward to $100K for information leading to Jazmine Barnes' killer" - khou.com, 1/2/19

lxxvii "Family of man wrongfully accused by activist Shaun King in Jazmine Barnes' shooting speaks out" - abc7chicago.com, 1/8/19

lxxviii "SayHerName" - Wikipedia.org

lxxix "An Update On The Sherita Dixon-Cole Story" - blackamericaweb.com, 5/22/18

lxxx "When the "victim" you fought for turns out to be the victimizer: Sherita Dixon-Cole and the painful consequences of a false report of sexual assault and police misconduct" - medium.com, 5/23/18

lxxxi "Jazmine Barnes' mom speaks out after suspects arrested in connection with deadly shooting" - abc13.com, 1/7/19

lxxxii "LOOK: The 49ers are slashing prices on Colin Kaepernick jerseys" - cbssports.com, 12/1/15

lxxxiii "Colin Kaepernick explains why he sat during national anthem" - 8/27/16

lxxxiv "Ruth Bader Ginsburg Says Colin Kaepernick's Protest Is 'Dumb'" - time.com, 10/10/16

lxxxv "Boomer Esiason 'disgusted' by Colin Kaepernick, calls QB a 'disgrace'" - nj.com, 8/30/16

lxxxvi "Mike Ditka on Colin Kaepernick's Protest: 'Get the Hell Out'" - nbcchicago.com, 9/24/16

lxxxvii "Drew Brees said he felt compelled to speak out against Colin Kaepernick's method of protest" - espn.com

lxxxviii "Victor Cruz to Colin Kaepernick: 'You've got to respect the flag'" - usatoday.com, 8/28/16

lxxxix "@JustinPugh" - twitter.com, 8/27/16

xc "Obama asks Kaepernick to think about pain he's causing military families" - politico.com, 9/28/16

xci "Colin Kaepernick on death threats: if I'm killed 'you've proved my point'" - theguardian.com, 9/20/16

xcii "NFL's TV Ratings Continue Slide Amidst National Anthem Protests" - forbes.com, 9/23/16

xciii "What the NFL Players' Union Chief Has to Say About Colin Kaepernick's Protest" - thenation.com, 8/27/16

xciv "Papa John slams NFL, blames national anthem protests for declining pizza sales" - commercialappeal.com, 11/1/17

xcv "Gaffes, TV ratings concerns dominated as NFL, players forged anthem peace" - espn.com, 10/27/17

xcvi "Houston Texans owner Bob McNair apologizes for "inmates running the prison" comment" - cbsnews.com, 10/27/17

xcvii "Mike Freeman's 10-Point Stance: Kaepernick Anger Intense in NFL Front Offices" - bleacherreport.com, 8/31/16

xcviii "Rae Carruth" - Wikipedia.org

xcix "Trump On Kaepernick: 'Maybe He Should Find A Country That Works Better For Him'" - buzzfeednews.com, 8/29/16

c "More than 200 NFL players sit or kneel during national anthem" - chicagotribune.com, 9/24/17

ci "Hillary Clinton's purse essential? Hot sauce" - washingtonpost.com

cii "Colin Kaepernick: Hillary Clinton Would Be In Prison If She Was Any Other Person" - youtube.com/NTKnetwork, 8/29/16

ciii "The official anthem of the RNC? 'Lock her up'" - ajc.com, 7/20/16

civ "Colin Kaepernick reportedly plans to opt out of final year of 49ers deal" - nydailynews.com, 2/3/17

cv "Should Giants sign Colin Kaepernick?" - giantswire.usatoday.com, 10/12/18

cvi "Black unemployment rate hits a record low" - money.cnn.com, 6/1/18

cvii "Donald Trump takes shot at Colin Kaepernick's free-agent status" - espn.com, 3/21/17

cviii "#NoKaepernickNoNFL - Boycott NFL Games If Colin Kaepernick Doesn't Play This Season" - change.org, cix "Spike Lee Signal-Boosts Rally for Still-Unsigned Colin Kaepernick at NFL HQ" - colorlines.com, 8/9/17

cx "Colin Kaepernick supporters demonstrate at NFL offices, call for boycott" - espn.com, 8/24/17

cxi "Source: Seahawks Canceled Kaepernick Workout Because He Wouldn't Agree to Stop Kneeling" - slate.com, 4/12/18

cxii "John Harbaugh: It's intellectually lazy to say Kaepernick is being blackballed" - cbssports.com, 3/28/17

cxiii "Michael Vick: Colin Kaepernick's problem is his play, not his protest" - profootballtalk.nbcsports.com, 7/17/17

cxiv "Michael Vick says Colin Kaepernick needs to cut his hair if he wants to be signed by an NFL team" - si.com, 7/17/17

cxv "Colin Kaepernick to stand during national anthem next season" - espn.com, 3/3/17

cxvi "NFL's Colin Kaepernick incorrectly credits Winston Churchill for quote about lies" - politifact.com, 10/9/17

cxvii "QB Colin Kaepernick files grievance for collusion against NFL owners" - espn.com, 10/16/17

cxviii "NFL Commissioner Roger Goodell: Kaepernick is not being blackballed over anthem protests" - cnbc.com, 12/11/17

cxix "NFL Players' Union Names Kaepernick 'Community MVP' For Charity Work"

cxx "Malcolm Jenkins: I'd hold anthem demonstration even if team's owner forbid it" - nbcsports.com, 10/9/17

cxxi "What protesting NFL players like me want to do next" - washingtonpost.com, 9/30/17

cxxii "The memo 4 players sent NFL commissioner Roger Goodell" - sports.yahoo.com, 9/20/17

cxxiii "Malcolm Jenkins, the new face of NFL player protests, says 'We're really just at the beginning'" - washingtonpost.com, 9/5/18

cxxiv "Josh Norman says he wasn't trying to 'tear down' Colin Kaepernick" - washingtonpost.com, 9/6/18

cxxv "Unsigned safety Eric Reid files collusion grievance against NFL" - espn.com, 5/2/18

cxxvi "Matthew 26:35" - King James Bible

cxxvii "What are the odds of the NFL 'randomly' drug-testing Eric Reid 7 times this season?" - sports.yahoo.com, 12/18/18

cxxviii "Irreconcilable differences: Why the Players Coalition split apart" - theundefeated.com, 2/2/18

cxxix "NFL, Players Coalition finalize social justice partnership" - nfl.com, 5/22/18

cxxx "Colin Kaepernick Pledges $1 Million to Charity as Anthem Protest Spreads" -nbcnews.com, 9/2/16

cxxxi "Irreconcilable differences: Why the Players Coalition split apart" - theundefeated.com, 2/2/18

cxxxii "Emails Show Colin Kaepernick Frozen Out of Discussions Between NFL Players and Owners" - slate.com, 10/29/18

cxxxiii "LeBron James rips NFL owners as 'old white men' with 'slave mentality'" - usatoday.com, 12/21/18

cxxxiv "'That was terrible': Stephen Curry didn't care for this week's Sports Illustrated Cover" - washingtonpost.com 9/27/17

cxxxv "Sports Illustrated Whitesplains Why It Left Colin Kaepernick Off 'Sports United' Cover" - theroot.com, 9/28/17

cxxxvi "The Thinking Behind SI's Controversial 'Sports United' Cover" - si.com, 9/26/17

cxxxvii "RedZone's @AndrewSiciliano" - twitter.com, 12/31/17

cxxxviii "Colin Kaepernick makes surprise appearance at 'Unthanksgiving Day' on Alcatraz" - sfgate.com, 11/23/17

cxxxix "@Kaepernick7" - twitter.com, 11/23/17

cxl "Colin Kaepernick lands million-dollar book deal" - pagesix.com, 10/24/17

cxli "J.J. Watt's Hurricane Harvey relief fund closes with over $37 million raised" - usatoday.com, 9/15/17

cxlii "Colin Kaepernick accepts Muhammad Ali Legacy Award from Beyoncé" - espn.com, 12/6/17

cxliii "Nike Nearly Dropped Colin Kaepernick Before Embracing Him" - nytimes.com, 9/26/18

cxliv "Jim Brown: Colin Kaepernick has to decide if he's an activist or a football player" - cbssports.com, 8/25/17

cxlv "@WhitlockJason" - Twitter.com, 9/3/18

cxlvi "Here's How Much Colin Kaepernick Will Make in His Controversial New Ad Deal With Nike, According to Sports Experts" - money.com, 9/4/18

cxlvii "Nike Will Be NFL's Uniform And Apparel Supplier For Forseeable Future After Long-Term Extension" - forbes.com, 3/27/18

cxlviii "Animal-Friendly Idioms That Your Students Will Love" - peta.org

cxlix "Nike has donated three times as much money to Republicans as Democrats this year" - sports.yahoo.com, 9/23/18

cl "People are destroying their Nike shoes and socks to protest Nike's Colin Kaepernick ad campaign" - businessinsider.com, 9/4/18

cli "Mobile Baptist pastor cuts up Nike gear during Sunday sermon" - al.com, 9/11/18

clii "College of the Ozarks drops Nike, will 'choose country over company'" - news-leader.com, 9/5/18 cliii "'It grossly insults the men and women who really do make sacrifices for the sake of our nation': Police organization calls for its 241,000 members to boycott Nike following the release of the company's controversial Colin Kaepernick ad" - dailymail.co.uk, 9/4/18

cliv "Louisiana town bans purchases of all Nike products" - sports.yahoo.com, 9/9/18

clv "Nike's Mark Parker says Colin Kaepernick ad leads to record engagement with brand" - espn.com, 9/25/18

clvi "Nike Premieres Kaep Merch and New Logo—and Sells Out Within Hours (But There's Still Hope)" - theglowup.theroot.com, 10/26/18

clvii "Former San Francisco 49ers quarterback and pioneer of NFL kneeling protest Colin Kaepernick files to trademark black-and-white image of his face and hair" - dailymail.co.uk, 10/10/18

clviii "Colin Kaepernick wins summary judgment case vs. NFL keeping grievance alive" - sports.yahoo.com, 8/30/18

clix "Colin Kaepernick reaches settlement in national anthem kneeling collusion case against NFL" - cnbc.com, 2/15/19

clx "Rihanna Declined Super Bowl LIII Halftime Show Offer in Support of Colin Kaepernick" - usmagazine.com, 10/18/18

clxi "Cardi B Refuses to Perform at the Super Bowl Halftime Show Until the NFL 'Hires Colin Kaepernick Back'" – 2/5/18

clxii "I Feel Pretty angry: Amy Schumer is refusing to participate in any Super Bowl ads in support of Colin Kaepernick's knee protest saying 'hitting the NFL with the advertisers is the only way to hurt them'" - dailymail.co.uk, 10/21/18

clxiii "The possibility of Beto O'Rourke's 2020 presidential run has donors thinking he's the 'new Barack Obama'" - businessinsider.com, 11/25/18

clxiv "'I can think of nothing more American': Beto O'Rourke responds to question on NFL protests – video" - theguardian.com, 8/22/18

clxv "@KingJames" – twitter.com, 8/23/18

clxvi "@TheEllenShow" – twitter.com, 8/22/18

clxvii "Cheerleader takes knee during anthem; 49ers silent" - mercurynews.com, 11/1/18

clxviii "Photos: 49ers vs. Packers All-time" - 49ers.com

clxix "49ers' Colin Kaepernick sets quarterback playoff rushing record" - nfl.com, 1/12/13

clxx "49ers apologize for Colin Kaepernick snub in photo gallery" - sports.yahoo.com, 10/13/18

clxxi "Colin Kaepernick Wins Amnesty International's Highest Honor" - time.com, 4/21/18

clxxii "Colin Kaepernick honored by ACLU, given award for courageous advocacy" - sports.yahoo.com, 12/4/17

clxxiii "@ThomasSowell" – twitter.com, 1/15/09

clxxiv "'Love is at the root of our resistance, and it will fortify everything we do': Colin Kaepernick receives Harvard black history award alongside Dave Chappelle" - dailymail.co.uk, 10/12/18

clxxv "Finlay: Colin Kaepernick 'best of the available options' as Redskins look to sign QB" - nbcsports.com, 12/4/18

clxxvi "Doug Flutie American Football Player" - britannica.com

clxxvii "The Alliance of American Football" – aaf.com

clxxviii "Colin Kaepernick reportedly demanded $20M to play for AAF" - sports.yahoo.com, 2/14/19

clxxix "Alliance of American Football releases salary details" - sports.yahoo.com, 7/12/18

clxxx "My Larger Education: Being Chapters from My Experience" – Booker T. Washington, 1911

clxxxi "Jesse Jackson Equates Millionaire NFL Players to Slaves 'Picking Cotton Balls'" -ijr.com

clxxxii "Matthew 16:18" – King James Version

Made in the USA
Coppell, TX
07 June 2020

27110347R00083